MARY:
MODEL OF JUSTICE

★ ★ ★

(Reflections On The Magnificat)

MARY:
MODEL OF JUSTICE

★ ★ ★

(Reflections On The Magnificat)

by

Rev. William F. Maestri

ALBA · HOUSE NEW · YORK

SOCIETY OF ST. PAUL, 2187 VICTORY BLVD., STATEN ISLAND, NEW YORK 10314

Library of Congress Cataloging in Publication Data

Maestri, William F.
  Mary, model of justice

  1. Magnificat — Criticism, interpretation, etc.
2. Mary, Blessed Virgin, Saint — Theology.   3. Justice
(Virtue) — Biblical teaching.   4. Sociology, Christian
(Catholic)   5. Catholic Church — Doctrines.   Title.
BS2595.2.M34   1987   226'.406   86-22304
ISBN 0-8189-0511-5

Nihil Obstat:
Rev. John H. Miller, C.S.C
Censor Librorum

Imprimatur:
Most Rev. Philip M. Hannan
Archbishop of New Orleans

Designed, printed and bound in the United States of
America by the Fathers and Brothers of the
Society of St. Paul, 2187 Victory Boulevard,
Staten Island, New York 10314, as part of their
communications apostolate.

---

2 3 4 5 6 7 8 9 (Current Printing: first digit)

Contents

Introduction

The Dogmatic Constitution on the Church (Lumen Gentium) devotes an entire chapter to The Blessed Virgin Mary ("The Role Of The Blessed Virgin Mary, Mother Of God In The Mystery Of Christ And The Church"). In section four ("Devotion to the Blessed Virgin in the Church") we read the following: "Mary was involved in the mysteries of Christ. As the most holy Mother of God she was, after her Son, exalted by divine grace above all angels and men. Hence the Church appropriately honors her with special reverence." These words about Mary may come as a surprise to many. For it is easy to get the impression, in our post-Vatican II Church, that Mary has been dismissed as obsolete or belongs to a simpler time; that Mary has little to say to the modern world of nuclear war, terrorism, and large multi-nationals; or that the Church has come of age and it is time to let go of Mary.

Such a view, while seeming to be accurate, is false. The Council Fathers clearly affirmed the importance of Mary for the spiritual growth of the Christian and the life of the Church as a whole. Not only did Mary endure in the documents of the Second Vatican Council, but she *continues* to exert a profound influence on the religious imagination and behavior of many Catholics (especially the young).

Father Andrew M. Greeley and his associates at the National Opinion Research Center (NORC) have gathered some interesting data on the influence of Mary on the religious imagination. Before sharing Father Greeley's findings one should consider the following statements:

> One of the more interesting phenomenon of continuity among American Catholics in the years since the Second Vatican Council has been the persistence of the importance of the Mary image in the religious imagination of Catholics. Young Catholics . . . between 15 and 30 had strong and influential images of Mary. (*American Catholics Since the Council. An Unauthorized Report* by Andrew M. Greeley, p. 102)

The persistence of Mary in the religious imagination is intertwined with the following forms of religious behavior:

— Those who have expressed Mary as an influence on their behavior indicate they are socially committed to economic and political justice;

— Mary has influenced their prayer life;

— Mary has heightened their awareness of the need for racial justice; and

— Mary is a powerful influence on sexual fulfillment in marriage.

What Father Greeley and his associates have found is quite simple: Mary has endured and is making a profound influence on the religious imagination and behavior of Catholics. The elites may have dismissed Mary but the Catholic in the market place keeps right on "bringing flowers to the rarest and fairest."

Furthermore, those who are high on the "Madonna scale" exhibit a deep sense of moral commitment in the area of sexual ethics. For they are more likely to reject abortion on demand and disapprove of pre-marital sex and living together than those who score low on the Madonna scale. Why? The answer seems to be as follows: those who score high on the scale relate to Mary as one who is kind, patient, loving, comforting, and gentle. Hence one builds up a relationship of trust and fidelity. This seems to *carry over* into the interpersonal realm. We come to treat others the way we experience Mary and we expect others to do likewise.

Not only has Mary been labeled (and libeled) as irrelevant but she has also been looked upon as an obstacle to ecumenical dialogue. Again Father Greeley's research and observations are key:

> We have no way of knowing how non-Catholics in general react to the Mary symbol. However, we can investigate the reactions of the non-Catholics who were married to our respondents. Rather surprisingly, Mary's image is almost as good with them as it is with Catholics . . . Mary may actually be an asset to ecumenism instead of a liability. (*American Catholics Since the Council*, p. 109)

The ecumenical appeal of Mary was beautifully captured in a work on Mary by the renowned biblical scholar Father Raymond E. Brown, S.S. and several other scholars both Catholic and Protestant. Father Brown and his group came to see how much they were united in their esteem for Mary. He wrote: "Yet we found we shared a common regard for 'the mother of Jesus', as the Fourth Gospel consistently entitles her. From the New Testament pictures of her we have learned afresh something of what faith and discipleship ought to mean within the family of God." (*Mary in the New Testament*, p. 6).

To recognize the importance of Mary in Scripture, tradition, and the everyday life of the Christian is not to overlook the abuses concerning mariology. Once again the words of the Second Vatican Council must be taken to heart:

> But this Synod earnestly exhorts theologians and preachers of the divine word that in treating of the unique dignity of the Mother of God, they carefully and equally avoid the falsity of exaggeration on the one hand, and the excess of narrow-

mindedness on the other . . . true devotion consists neither in
fruitless and passing emotion, nor in a certain vain credulity.
Rather, it proceeds from true faith, by which we are led to
know the excellence of the Mother of God, and are moved to a
filial love toward our mother and to the imitation of her
virtues. (*Dogmatic Constitution on the Church*, ch. 8, p. 95)

Without question Mary has been abused by conservative and
liberal extremists. However, we must keep in mind that abuses are
not sufficient arguments against the proper use of something. True
devotion to Mary leads us ultimately to Jesus Christ. Mary's whole
life was one of enfleshing the Word and being a true servant to the
World. Mary is the first Christian and the model of what it means to
follow Jesus. The Church esteems Mary because she left us an
enduring example of what it means to be a disciple and a community of disciples — making Jesus present. Pope Paul VI put it
beautifully:

The Virgin Mary has always been proposed to the faithful by
the Church as an example to be imitated, not precisely in the
type of life she led, and much less for the socio-cultural
background in which she lived and which today scarcely exists
anywhere. Rather she is held up as an example to the faithful
for the way in which by her own particular life she fully and
responsibly accepted the will of God, because she heard the
word of God and did it, and because charity and the spirit of
service were the driving forces of her actions. She is worthy of
imitation because she was, the first and most perfect of Christ's
disciples. (*Marialis Cultus*, Feb., 1974)

It is because Mary heard *and* acted on God's Word in the spirit
of service that she is the model of justice. Far from removing the
Christian from the concerns of the poor and oppressed, Mary
inspires us to be as much for others as we are for ourselves. The

honoring of Mary need not diminish our hungering and thirsting for justice. Just the opposite is true. By holding Mary in high regard we are challenged to make the cries of the poor our own. Hence it is not surprising that devotion to Mary is so powerful among the poor in third-world Latin American countries. Harvard theologian Harvey Cox has written:

> When one ponders this question [can popular piety advance liberation?] it is hard not to consider the many popular images of Mary. Indeed, in recent years some feminists who began by rejecting popular mariology as a male-devised means of social control have begun to see certain virgin goddesses as positive symbols of women. . . What a cosmic paradox! It might turn out to be a key ingredient in the liberation of women and in the formulation of a post modern and post sexist theology. (*Religion in the Secular City*, p. 256)

Of special interest is the image of Mary as Our Lady of Guadalupe. This image or story of Mary contains the three basic themes of liberation according to Professor Cox: the Guadalupe Lady is dark-skinned and highlights the dignity of people of color. This Lady is a woman who represents the ''second sex'' and speaks of the liberation of women everywhere. And thirdly, Our Lady of Guadalupe is a poor person and shares fellowship with the wretched of the earth. While deeply appreciative of Professor Cox's insights I would make one modification. Mary speaks of the need to liberate *all* persons who find themselves in bondage to sin (personal and collective). There can be no true freedom if the oppressor and the master are not redeemed. The goal of liberation is achieved through reconciliation and love. In a profound sense there can be no authentic women's liberation that does not include men. Mary liberates all people to do God's will as members of His family.

A very important theme that is present throughout the documents of the Second Vatican Council is the need for the Christian (and the Church as a whole) to develop a faith that does justice. In the past two decades we have witnessed the development of various theological perspectives which highlight the importance of justice for the Christian life. The Council Fathers wrote: "Christians who take an active part in modern socio-economic development and defend justice and charity should be convinced that they can make a great contribution to the prosperity of mankind and the peace of the world. Whether they do so as individuals or in association, let their example be a shining one." (*Pastoral Constitution on the Church in the Modern World*). Unfortunately this call to justice was interpreted by some to mean that all traditional forms of spirituality and piety were to be abandoned. Devotion to Mary was often singled out as a prime example. It seemed that one could not esteem Mary and be concerned about the poor and oppressed.

Nothing could have been further from the truth. The thesis of this book will advance the following claim: the celebrating of what God has done for Mary and a faith that does justice are powerfully connected. Mary is a woman of God's justice and a powerful disclosure model for the Church and the individual Christian. How do we know this? By turning to the pages of Scripture. Father Karl Rahner, S.J. has written:

> When a Catholic wants to reflect more deeply on the mystery of the blessed Virgin, the first thing he does is to open Holy Scripture and see what it has to say about the blessed Virgin Mother of our Lord Jesus Christ. . . The Church preaches precisely what she has read unceasingly throughout the centuries; we too can repeat what the faith of the Church keeps on affirming concerning Mary. (*Mary Mother of the Lord*, by Karl Rahner, S.J., pp. 21-22.)

Father Rahner is not suggesting that our contact with Mary comes first and only through Scripture. We come to know "this woman for others" through our mother — our woman for us. We learn about Mary through stories, images, and the preaching we hear. Furthermore, the significance of Mary has been raised to the level of dogmatic teachings. The Church, through the magisterium, holds that Mary provides an official and public example of putting God's work into action. And Mary's life (birth, ministry, death, and assumption) is a model and inspiration as to what God desires for each of us.

In the brief reflections that are contained in this book we want to center our efforts on the Magnificat found in the Gospel of Luke. These ten short verses (Lk 1:46-55) will provide the biblical basis for our reflections on Mary as the model of justice. The format of what follows is rather simple. There are five chapters each centering on a different aspect of the Magnificat and how it relates to justice in the life of Mary. The five major themes are joy, holiness, mercy, power, and memory. The book closes with an epilogue and a selected bibliography which will provide, hopefully, a listing of books for further reading. Naturally, throughout our reflections, we will relate the themes of the Magnificat, the pursuit of justice, and the life of Mary to our own lives.

One of Mary's most attractive qualities is her deep sense of gratitude. Hence a book about Mary should exhibit this quality by the author. There are many to thank: I am indebted to Fathers Victor and Timothy of the Society of St. Paul / Alba House. Gratitude is extended to the communities which allow me to teach and write: St. Joseph Seminary College, Mercy Academy, and St. Scholastica Academy. Without the expert typing of Beth J. Duke, the manuscript would not have reached its final form. Finally, I am grateful to Mary the Mother of Jesus. This book is a very inadequate expression of my thankfulness.

William F. Maestri
St. Joseph Abbey
Solemnity of the Mother of God, 1987

Into our hands
Mary has given her child:
heir to the world's tears,
heir to the world's toil,
heir to the world's scars,
heir to the chill dawn
over the ruin of wars.

She has laid Love in His cradle,
answering for us all:
"Be it done unto me:" . . .

(THE REED
by Caryll Houselander)

MARY:
MODEL OF JUSTICE

★ ★ ★

(Reflections On The Magnificat)

CHAPTER

1

Joy And Justice

"My soul magnifies the Lord, and my spirit rejoices in God my savior, for he has regarded the low estate of his handmaid."
(Lk 1:46-48)

Before we begin our reflections on the Magnificat a word must be said about the Gospel of Luke in general. It is one of the most appealing of biblical writings. Luke not only challenges the taken-for-granted values of the day concerning right and wrong; good and bad; but he also highlights the most uncelebrated of his day to be heroes and heroines for the Kingdom. Hence sinners, the poor, and women play key roles in his Gospel. How inadequate our story of Jesus would be without Luke!

If the Gospel of John highlights the importance of the Incarnation — the Word becoming flesh — then it is Luke who reminds us that the Word becomes poor, rejected, and lowly flesh. These have a special place in the ministry of Jesus and the Kingdom. Among the many objections raised against Jesus, a favorite is his troubling habit of enjoying table-fellowship with "sinners." The self-righteous folk extend the category "sinner" to include social outcasts, Samaritans and gentiles, tax collectors, and even Jews who do not obey the whole of the law. Why is Jesus found among such an assortment of despised? Jesus' answer is simple: they are in need of a physician. They need someone to love and accept them. It is the sinner who is most in need of table-fellowship with Jesus so they may know that God's love is enduring and life-giving. With God it is always possible to begin anew. The rejection by the respectable folk does not correspond to God's rejection. On the contrary. Jesus tells His audience (and us) that God is a Loving, Forgiving Father whose love searches out the lost and brings home the wayward. God's love brings life to the one who was given up for dead. And above all, God is a God who must celebrate each time one of His children comes to their senses. Luke's story of God is one in which one lost sheep and one lost sinner *MUST* be found. God will not rest. And finally, Jesus is a Messiah whose ministry from start to finish centers around forgiving love. It is Luke's Jesus whose final act before he dies is forgiveness and new life: "Truly, I say to you, today you will be with me in Paradise" (Lk 23:43).

Throughout the Gospel of Luke we never lose sight of the fact that Jesus is poor. Jesus shares a special kinship with the economically poor for He is one of them. There is about Luke a genuinely radical call to poverty by *all* who wish to follow Jesus: "Fear not, little flock, for it is your Father's good pleasure to give you the kingdom. Sell your possessions, and give alms; provide yourselves with purses that do not grow old, with a treasure in the heavens that does not fail, where no thief approaches and no moth destroys. For where your treasure is, there will your heart be also" (Lk 12:32-34). Biblical scholar Alois Stoger has written the following:

> . . . Luke presents Jesus as the savior of those who were most in need of saving, the poor. . . By almsgiving the Christian enters into the sympathy of Jesus for the poor and helpless. . . Assisting the poor by occasional or even frequent donations is

not enough; the generosity of Christians should drive them to the point where conditions are equalized. If wealth cannot be perfectly shared, poverty can. (*New Testament For Spiritual Reading*, Edited by John L. McKenzie, S.J. Volume I. "The Gospel According to St. Luke" by Alois Stoger)

On the above quoted passage from Luke's Gospel, Alois Stoger writes with insight: "Jesus' disciples form a little flock. . . Despite their limited numbers, their insignificance, powerlessness, and poverty, God will give them His kingdom, a power and a dominion which surpass all other kingdoms." The richness of this "little flock" does not come from the agenda of the world, but from the Father's abiding love. When one abides in God there is no need to be anxious.

Women occupy a special place in the Gospel of Luke and the ministry of Jesus. This should not surprise us, considering that women were an oppressed class. Women were part of the poor. They did not have the "clout" of men in religion and politics. Unlike the Gospel of Matthew in which Joseph is the major character in the infancy narrative, Luke's infancy narrative places Mary front and center. Martha and Mary provide hospitality and support for Jesus and his ministry. The poor widow mentioned in Lk 21:1-4 is praised by Jesus for her generosity and trust in God. Women follow Jesus to his crucifixion and death. Women go to the tomb of Jesus to care for his body. What they find is an empty tomb. And they receive the message that Jesus is not to be found among the dead. These women (Mary Magdalene, Joanna, and Mary the mother of James and the other women) in turn told the apostles who refused to believe them (another example of male superiority!). Luke highlights the ways in which women minister to Jesus as he calls *all* people to respond to the Kingdom.

The Magnificat: An Overview

Biblical scholars tell us that the Magnificat is one of four canticles contained in the Lucan infancy narrative: the Magnificat (1:46-55), the Benedictus (1:67-79), the Gloria in Excelsis (2:13-14), and the Nunc Dimittis (2:28-32). There are a number of theories concerning the composition of these canticles ranging from the uncritical position which attributes authorship to the one who proclaims it to the position which holds that Luke composed them all. The noted Catholic biblical scholar Father Raymond E. Brown, S.S. holds that the canticles were pre-Lucan and added by Luke to an already existing Lucan narrative. These pre-existing canticles were of Jewish Christian composition.

Father Brown's extensive research on the infancy narratives in Matthew and Luke is contained in his remarkable book, *The Birth of the Messiah.* In his discussion of the Magnificat, Father Brown indicates that it is similar to the psalm type known as the hymn of praise. Each has three basic parts: the introduction praising God; the body of the hymn indicating why God should be praised; and the concluding section which once again recounts the motive for praise along with a blessing and/or petition for a need on behalf of the individual or the nation. It is in the Magnificat that the oppressed (but blessed or fortunate) individual (Mary) is joined with the oppressed community (Israel) in offering a hymn of praise. Far from oppression turning to self-pity or violence, the oppressed are blessed by God, strengthened, and lift up their voices in praising Him from generation to generation.

Mary: Unself-Centered/God-Centered

The opening words of the Magnificat beautifully capture the essence of Mary's life: "My soul magnifies the Lord." Mary's entire life was one of being open to and magnifying the presence of the Lord. From the moment of her immaculate conception to her glorious assumption, Mary sought to enlarge the grace of God and decrease the influence of her own ego. In many ways Mary is akin to John the Baptist: they both are unselfish so that Jesus can become more present. Yet it is in decreasing the ego that both Mary and the Baptist become what they really are — heralds of the true Messiah. Those absorbed in self soon turn God into an extension of the ego. The self-centered make God into their own image. The God-centered are transformed into the Divine image. Luther, meditating on the Magnificat, wrote:

> Mary sang, "My soul doth magnify the Lord" — not herself, but the Lord. She was Queen of Queens, Virgin of Virgins, Mother of Mothers, but she despised no man. "True it is," she said, "I am blessed, but I do not magnify myself; my soul doth magnify the Lord. What I am, I am through His grace, which He has bestowed upon me, unworthy as I am." Here we have the highest joy and still humility; honor and subjection not only toward God but also toward men. (*Luther's Meditations on the Gospel*, by Roland H. Bainton)

This last sentence is crucial. The magnifying of the Lord does not turn Mary away from others. Quite the contrary. It is because she has allowed, in faith and freedom, God to fill her heart that Mary can risk being for others. To be rich in the ways of God is an invitation to fellowship with others. Mary does not turn the gift of God into a self-centered possession or an excuse for not loving others. When God's grace stretches a soul, one becomes more attentive to the needs of others. Mary's magnifying the Lord means that God works *through* her. Mary is the model for the disciple and the Church. The annunciation to Mary is followed by her visitation to Elizabeth so as to rejoice with her kinswoman. Luke tells us after the Magnificat that "Mary remained with Elizabeth about three months and then returned home" (Lk 1:56). Mary *continues* to magnify God by her love and concern for Elizabeth.

These opening words of Mary are counter-cultural. For we know how easily we magnify and proclaim ourselves. In a culture of narcissism and me-ism the idea of being for others and God is both absurd and frightening. Self-absorption is not new. Our first parents were not satisfied to be creatures; they had to be like the gods (self-sufficient and self-made). The result is that we become less than what we are meant to be. American society is prone to self-absorption. Alexis de Tocqueville wrote in *Democracy in America*: "Each critizen is habitually engaged in the contemplation of a very puny object, namely himself." More recently, Alexander Solzhenitsyn in 1978 addressed "cultured despisers" at Harvard University. His words had the ring of an Old Testament prophet: "We have placed too much hope in politics and social reforms, only to find out that we were being deprived of our most precious possession: our spiritual life. It is trampled by the party mob in the East, by the commercial one in the West." In other words, the challenge of modern man is not only political and economic but fundamentally *spiritual*. The soul must once again magnify God so that egoism and pride can be transformed into a personal and national life that does justice.

To magnify the Lord does not come easy. Martin Luther in his commentary on the Magnificat highlights two dangers or approaches which disturb proper praise of God. The first type are those who refuse to praise the Lord unless the Lord showers them with good things — constantly. There is no room for the sword of love that must pierce the heart. Psalm 49 captures this well: "He will praise You when You shall do well to him" (verse 18). God falls from grace as soon as trouble comes and the cross appears on the horizon. The second type receive good things but assume it is because of their merit or worth. The soul of such people does not magnify the Lord but their own egos are enlarged. They assume that God owes them these good things in justice. It is easy to become self-righteous and filled with *pride*. This easily leads to an arrogance which separates one from God and neighbor. We really do not need Jesus for we believe we save ourselves. We despise others as being unworthy of our love.

Martin Luther offers an instructive illustration contrasting Mary with these false approaches to praising God. One day a godly woman was attending Mass when she had a vision. In the vision there were three virgins seated near the altar. A beautiful boy jumped from the altar and went to each virgin. To the first he was lavish in kindness, love, and compassion. To the second, the boy was not as attentive but he did show some kindness. To the third the boy was most cruel and vicious. Luther interprets the story in the following way: the first virgin represents the person who will only praise God when all is well. There is no room for costly grace. The second virgin represents our willingness to follow Jesus *up to a point*. However, there is a point beyond which we will not go. There are limits. Finally, the third virgin loves and praises God for His sheer goodness though she never directly experiences it. She loves God for Himself. This wise virgin is one who praises God in season and out of season; in time of abundance and in time of suffering.

These opening words of Mary are an insight into her whole life. Mary is anything but self-absorbed. She magnifies the Lord by allowing Him to work through her. It would have been easy for her to be proud and self-righteous. God's gifts could have occasioned her downfall. Yet this is not the case. Mary continues to be mindful of her poor, needful and lowly condition so that God can be magnified. Her great role in salvation history serves to draw her more deeply into love with God and others. Mary's life is one of saying, ''I seek not Thine, but Thee; Thou art to me no dearer when it goes well with me, nor any less dear when it goes ill.''

Rejoicing In The Savior

God is not only Lord but also Savior. And it is in the Savior that Mary experiences a joy which the world cannot give or take away. The world offers us a number of generic substitutes for joy: fanatical zeal, enthusiasm, and gloomy spirituality from which St. Teresa of Avila prayed to be delivered. To experience the presence of the Savior is to know true joy. Such knowledge is not acquired by willing or through intellectual powers. To know God as Savior and the subsequent joy that follows is to open to the Savior. God constantly searches for us. It is we who hide and flee. God continually searches for the lost sheep and the child who travels to a distant land. Karl Barth puts it beautifully:

> Joy is the most rare, the most scarce commodity in the world. . . In God my Savior when we have found Him or when He has found us, we rejoice, says Mary. The Savior will always be He who finds us at the end of our way, at the end of our scramblings and our flights, at the end of our optimism and pessimism. There where we only know one thing, that is this: I am lost unless He helps me. (*The Great Promise*, by Karl Barth, p. 47)

How hard it is for us moderns to rejoice in God our Savior! For it is part of the worldly wisdom that we are in need of no Savior outside ourselves. And even if there were a God He is indifferent to the events of history. No, we have come of age and must pull our own strings and be self-sufficient. Anything else is bad faith (Sartre), projections of importance (Feinbach), false consciousness (Marx), and baby-talk from the infantile personality (Freud). Yet Mary's words are part of the Divine Foolishness that confounds worldly wisdom. Mary is one like us in all aspects of our humanity. From her we learn that to be human is to be needful and dependent. We cannot be Savior to ourselves. We need a Redeemer who becomes our *poor* flesh in order to heal, strengthen, and make whole. The Savior that evokes true joy in Mary is not some Uncaused Cause or Prime Mover. Still less is this Savior the

Ground of Being or an Eternal Form. The Savior is One who causes our hearts to leap for joy.

The opening line of the Magnificat prepares us for what is to follow. God is one who takes note of the lowly. However, before we examine the second part of the opening verses we must keep in mind that Mary magnifies the Lord and rejoices in the Savior *before* He has done anything for her. Her response is not an example of reciprocity but one of rejoicing and praising God for Himself alone. The truly poor, naked, powerless, marginals, and wretched of the earth wait upon the Lord. And they are not disappointed. All that Mary and the lowly receive comes from God as pure gift. There is no room for pride — just gratitude and joy.

Mary: The One Of Low Estate

The God who is Lord and Savior is one who *cares* and is *involved* with His creation. God makes Himself known through creation, liberation, redemption, and abiding presence. God does not create and withdraw but is *active* in history calling all things to Himself. God makes Himself known as the Liberator in the Exodus experience. God guides His people from slavery to freedom. However, bondage is more than political and economic oppression. God's people must contend against the principalities and powers of sin and death. The God who is I AM is also the One on the Cross who is Suffering Servant and Abandoned One. The God who lives in unapproachable light empties Himself of glory and becomes like us. He assumes our condition — a slave — and through His death we are restored to eternal life. Our God becomes poor so that He can share in the poverty of our condition.

A question arises of utmost importance: Why does God favor the poor? Why does God show a bias (preference or what the Vatican's latest statement concerning liberation theology terms a *special love*) for the lowly and rejected? What is the significance of the oppressed in the eyes of God? The biblical witness is very powerful and clear: if God does not act on behalf of the poor and wretched, no one will. The poor will perish if God does not hear their cry and respond to their need. The condition of material poverty does *not* confer a special spiritual grace in and of itself, but poverty affords God an opportunity to teach us what His will and reign are about — *JUSTICE*. The God of the Bible is a God of *JUSTICE*.

The biblical *experience* (as opposed to an intellectual definition) of justice is fundamentally a statement about God and His action in history. There are two Hebrew words for justice: *sedaqah* and *mispat*. These words convey a sense of generosity, abundance, and gift. Justice is far from a balancing of scales and giving in hope of return. Justice is never based on mere merit but looks to *needs*. Hence the second aspect of justice (*mispat*) concerns itself with deliverance and breaking the yoke of slavery and oppression. God acts to bring relief by breaking the chains that imprison. He releases the fetters of those in bondage. God's justice demands that His people be set free. Justice is the affirmative action of God on behalf of those who have no one to plead their cause. Consider the words of Psalm 146:

> The Lord sets the prisoners free; the Lord opens the eyes of the blind. The Lord lifts up those who are bowed down; the Lord loves the righteous. The Lord watches over the sojourners, He upholds the widow and the fatherless; but the way of the wicked He brings to ruin. (vv. 7-9)

Biblical scholar and ethicist Stephen Charles Mott reminds us that God's justice or righteousness is never punishment for sin. It is action for the innocent and the broken-hearted who are special to God:

> Justice may then represent God's victory for the innocent or the oppressed, the negative side of which is the defeat of the

wicked or the oppressors, often described with terms other than those of justice. But our point is not that biblical justice is never punitive but rather that it is not restricted to the function. Justice is also vindication, deliverance, and creation of community. (*Biblical Ethics and Social Change*, by Stephen Charles Mott, p. 63)

The God of a justice that is generous and liberating has regard for "the low estate of his handmaid" Mary. For the Magnificat identifies Mary as one of the poor and lowly that are special to God. Mary is a member of the *Anawim*. What does this mean? The word itself comes from the Hebrew *anaw* along with its cognate *ani* which denotes the "poor, afflicted, humble." The Anawim are the poor and lowly. The word designates *both* those who are physically poor as well as those who relied totally on the gracious (just) presence of God. The opposite of the Anawim are those who rely on their own resources and power. They are the self-sufficient and self-made ones who believe they are what they possess. And what they possess comes only through their own efforts or merits. There is little or no room for gratitude. Pastor and theologian Eugene H. Peterson writing on the illusion of self-sufficiency puts it thusly:

We do not begin life on our own. We do not finish it on our own. Life, especially when we experience by faith the complex interplay of creation and salvation, is not fashioned out of our own genetic lumber and cultural warehouses. It is not hammered together with the planks and nails of our thoughts and dreams, our feelings and fancies. We are not self-sufficient. We enter a world that is created by God, that already has a rich history and is crowded with committed participants. . . We keep on being surprised because we are in on something beyond our management, something over our needs. (*Earth & Altar: The Community of Prayer in a Self-Bound Society*, by Eugene H. Peterson, p. 149)

The Anawim, ''the Poor Ones'', occupy a special place in the Gospel of Luke and the ministry of Jesus. In Lk 6:20 Jesus begins the Sermon on the Plain with the following words:

Blest are you poor; the reign of God is yours.
Blest are you who hunger; you shall be filled.
Blest are you who are weeping; you shall laugh.

Even before this, Jesus inaugurated his public ministry with the words of Isaiah the prophet:

The spirit of the Lord is upon me;
therefore He has anointed me.
He has sent me to bring glad tidings to the poor,
Recovery of sight to the blind
and release to prisoners,
To announce a year of favor from the Lord.
(Lk 4:18-19)

In an age of self-glory and the marketing personality Mary identifies herself as a member of the ''Poor Ones'' of the Lord. She is a handmaid of low estate through whom God will do wondrous things. As always it is God who is to be praised and glorified. God works through human weakness and poverty so as to confound the proud and turn to foolishness earthly wisdom. The God who cares for His ''poor ones'' has chosen a poor one to be the human instrument in which the Word will become poor flesh. Karl Barth reflecting on Mary's low estate writes:

Thus it is clear that God is a God of the poor, a God of those who are in need, who are there beneath, deeply beneath. How should it be otherwise if He is the Savior? But just because of this, that He regards the low estate of His handmaiden, He shows himself as a gracious God; as He who is good to us with a kindness which presupposes nothing, which knows the condition we are in and yet which comes to our aid. (*The Great Promise*, by Karl Barth, p. 47)

Concluding Remarks

The opening lines of the Magnificat are a powerful, abiding reminder of the truth of our human condition and the place of the poor in God's heart. We are all poor. And the poorest of the poor are those who live with the illusion of self-sufficiency and self-mastery. The life of Mary is one that teaches us to live without these illusions so as to be truly rich in God's grace. The poverty of our condition is not a cause for self-hatred or pretensions at omnipotence. In the presence of the God who became our poor flesh so we might become rich, we too can magnify the Lord. The graciousness of God is everywhere: friends, family, work, the gifts of creation, and yes, even our crosses. All of these are constant reminders of the everyday presence of God. There is no need for anger or resentment. We, like Mary, can rejoice in the Lord for who He is — our Lord and Savior — and what He has done for us and continues to do.

The Magnificat of Mary also places her with the "poor ones" of Yahweh. She is of low estate: a woman, poor, and a virgin (this we shall discuss in greater detail in a subsequent chapter). Mary stands in solidarity with all those who must wait upon the Lord. The life of Mary echoes the words of Judith in the Old Testament: "God is a God of the humble, a helper for the lowly, and support for the weak, a protector for those who are rejected, a savior for those who are in despair" (Jdt 9:11). Mary does not carry "clout" nor does she have access to the articles of worldly power and privilege. She is among the uncelebrated and ignored. Yet it is in just such a one that God is most capable of effecting His loving will. One can only respond with joyful gratitude.

In our next chapter we will examine the relationship between justice (which is understood to be generosity in the biblical sense) and holiness. A faith that does justice transcends humanistic ideals, socio-political programs for a Great Society, and a kind of simplistic call for redistribution of scarce goods. The call to live justly and walk humbly with God requires conversion — a change of heart. And when the human heart is changed so will the social heart be changed from stone to flesh. The Magnificat of Mary is not frozen in time but continues through all generations.

Holiness And Justice

"Behold, henceforth all generations will call me blessed; for
He who is mighty has done great things for me, and holy is His
name." (Lk 1:48-49)

The Magnificat recounts a number of God's more important
characteristics: He is mighty, merciful and His name is holy. One
of the most awe-inspiring scenes in all of Scripture is the call of the
prophet Isaiah:

In the year that King Uzziah died I saw the Lord sitting upon a
throne, high and lifted up; and His train filled the temple.
Above Him stood the seraphim; each had six wings: with two
they covered their faces, and with two they covered their feet,
and with two they flew. And one called to another and said:

"Holy, holy, holy is the Lord
of hosts; the whole earth is
full of his glory."

And the doorposts and the thresholds shook at the voice of
him who called, and the house was filled with smoke. (Is 6:1-4)

What is the meaning of the divine holiness? The holiness of God denotes the very nature or essence of God; it is not so much defined as experienced through God's action. The German theologian Rudolf Otto has written a classic book on holiness entitled *The Idea of the Holy*. Professor Otto holds that the divine both fascinates and repels. In the divine presence we are aware of our sinfulness. The above quoted passage from Isaiah goes on to record the prophet saying, "Woe is me! For I am lost; I am a man of unclean lips, and I dwell in the midst of people of unclean lips . . ." (Is 6:5). Yet Isaiah will also accept the mission to preach repentance to a nation gone astray: "And I heard the voice of the Lord saying, 'Whom shall I send, and who will go for me?' Then I said, 'Here am I! Send me' " (Is 6:8).

The holiness of God is not only displayed in visions to prophets but in His mighty deeds: liberation, restoration, and covenant fidelity. The God of the Bible is *active* in history constantly working to liberate people from the bondage of sin and those social structures which trample on human dignity. The story of the Exodus is the prime example of a God who cares for His people. And God *continues* to challenge and liberate the Israelites. God remembers the covenant even when Israel forgets and plays the harlot by chasing false gods. God's faithfulness will not be undermined by the faults of Israel. James H. Cone, a leading prophet of Black Theology, has written:

> It seems clear to me that whatever else we may say about Scripture, it is first and foremost a story of Israelite people who believed that Yahweh was involved in their history. In the Old Testament, the story begins with the first Exodus of Hebrew slaves from Egypt and continues through the second Exodus from Babylon and the rebuilding of the temple . . . the impact of the biblical message is clear on this point: God's salvation is revealed in the liberation of slaves from socio-political

bondage. ("What is Christian Theology?", by James H. Cone in *Scripture Bulletin*, Vol. XII. No. III Summer, 1982)

The holiness of Yahweh is not only experienced in His deliverance and restoration of Israel but in the demands of social justice placed *on* Israel. His holiness is above all just (generous). Israel, the people of the covenant, must be holy and just as Yahweh is. The book of Exodus leaves no doubt as to what is expected of Israel: "You shall not ill-treat any widow or fatherless child. If you do, be sure that I will listen if they appeal to Me. My anger will be roused and I will kill you with the sword" (Ex 22:23-24). These words are both prophetic and turn out to be a major theme of the prophets: Israel will never prosper at the expense of the poor and the powerless. God cannot be bought off with sacrifices and great liturgies. Yahweh's holiness demands justice: "I hate, I despise your feasts, and I take no delight in your solemn assemblies. . . Take away from Me the noise of your songs; to the melody of your harps I will not listen. But let justice roll down like waters, and righteousness like an overflowing stream" (Am 5:21, 23-24).

The holiness of Yahweh is experienced in His concern for the poor, weak, orphan, widow, and the dispossessed of the earth. Mary can say, "Holy is His name" because she, "a Poor One" (Anawim), has been looked upon in her lowliness and poverty. The New Testament does not invalidate the commitment of Yahweh to the poor but intensifies it. For God becomes our poor flesh in the Virgin Mary. Jesus goes about preaching the good news of salvation for all people. However, the self-righteous and powerful reject such news and put the preachers to death. This is always the response of the world to the holiness and graciousness of God. However, it is the poor, sinners, and rejected who open their hearts to Jesus. The political and religious leaders cannot endure his words any longer, so he is placed on a cross. The cross becomes God's total identification with the powerless and abandoned. Yet the cross gives way to the empty tomb and the victory of the resurrection. God overcomes the powers of oppression, injustice, and death through the victory of life, love, and hope. The holiness of God always seeks reconciliation and healing. The poor must know that they *are not* less in His eyes because they *have* less. The rich must know they *are not* more in His eyes because they *have* more. Once again Professor Cone: ''The Incarnation then is simply God taking upon the divine self human suffering and humiliation. The resurrection is the divine victory over suffering, the bestowal of freedom on all who are weak and helpless.'' The lowly hand-maid of the Lord plays an essential role in the Word becoming poor flesh and the victory of God's holy justice.

Conversion: A Change Of Heart

The crucial question for each person is: Who is your Lord? Who is the One that defines your existence and lights up your life? To whom do you give ultimate allegiance? Mary's answer is unequivocal: ultimate devotion is given to the God who has done great things for her. It is the God who liberates and cares for the poor and those of low esteem. Yet Mary's answer is as much in dispute today as it was in her own day. The Lordship of Yahweh-Jesus is a disputed Lordship. There are many challengers for our devotion: money, power, popularity, sex, and beauty. How are we to smash the idols so as to worship the living God in spirit and truth?

The Bible speaks continually about the need for conversion (*metanoia*). Just what is this? Coversion is more than a mere resolution or promise to try harder or ''be a better person.'' It is a total change in the way one values, judges, and exists in the world. Conversion requires a giving up of the old, secure patterns of behavior and the taking on a whole new way of being-in-the-world. It is the turning away from the illusion of self-sufficiency and the idols of destruction to the living God of the covenant. Such a radical change in one's life direction is beautifully captured in the book of Hosea.

The prophet Hosea is called to preach to the northern kingdom (Israel). The central theme of his preaching is the ultimate victory of God's redeeming, forgiving love. The divine love is at the center of all conversion and change. The human heart can be changed because God's love prepares the way. Hosea marries a harlot and suffers much from her infidelity. Yet he remains faithful and will not abandon his commitments. So it is with Yahweh. God is in a covenant (marriage) with Israel who plays the harlot. Israel's infidelity will not discourage Yahweh. He will continue to love Israel as Hosea loves his unfaithful wife Gomer. God is tempted to use His power to shame and destroy Israel. But this He will not do, for He is a God of persuasive love not violence. In one of the most beautiful passages in Scripture we read:

> Therefore, behold I will allure her, and bring her into the wilderness, and speak tenderly to her . . . and there she shall respond as in the days of her youth, as at the time when she came out of the land of Egypt . . . and I will betroth you to Me for ever; I will betroth you to Me in righteousness and in justice, in steadfast love, and in mercy. I will betroth you to Me in faithfulness; and you shall know the Lord. (Ho 2:14-15, 19-20)

The story and preaching of Hosea contains one of the most important biblical insights: God acts through love and the living presence of His grace. A true and lasting conversion does not come through fear and oppression. The God of liberation acts by love. The God of the poor and the lowly never resorts to the tactics of the mighty. We can turn to God because God has turned to us in love.

Conversion or change never remains personal or a habit of the heart. It has profound social consequences. Conversion, like love, cannot be cloistered to the realm of face to face relationships. Reinhold Niebuhr once wrote, "The effort to confine *agape* to the love of personal relations and to place all structures and artifices of justice outside that realm makes Christian love irrelevant to the problems of man's common life'' (*Christian Realism and Political Problems*, p. 167). The words of Niebuhr apply to conversion as well. Conversion must critique the social structures of our common life. If this is not done, our biblical faith becomes a monument to irrelevancy. The political, social, and economic spheres are not immune from the invitation to repent.

The need for social or structural conversion challenges much in our culture and certain forms of spirituality. Culturally American society is what the noted historian Henry Steele Commager calls ''the empire of reason.'' America has embodied the ideals of the Enlightenment and the political philosophy of liberalism (social contract). What has been the social construction of reality? We Americans highly prize the values of instrumental rationalism and individual freedom. We extol the virtues of individual rights and the uniqueness of the individual. Above all we prize the *private*. Privacy has become one of the most sought after badges in modern society. However, this freedom, individualism, and privacy have not been gained without a price. Professor Stanley Hauerwas writes, ''In the name of freedom we have created 'the individual' who now longs for community in the form of 'interpersonal interaction' '' (*A Community of Character*, p. 160). Free, calculating, and private modern man is also lonely and is seeking what Christopher Lasch calls a ''haven in a heartless world.'' Even our most intimate relationships seem to lack something — a deep commitment based on a shared life-story or narrative. We live, *move*, and have our being in a world too often surrounded by ''friendly strangers'' who make no demands and who have no expectations. Life is nothing more than a contract between consenting individuals who seek their private self-interests.

The obstacles for social conversion extend beyond a culture which is highly private, self-interested, competitive, calculating, and lonely. Christian spirituality has not always been friendly to the social dimensions of the Gospel and the reality of social sin. Too often Christian spirituality has fallen into a spiritual*ism* which reduced our relationship to God to a simple "Thee and Me." The problems of the neighbor and of oppressive social structures were ignored. Yet any authentic God-talk and spirituality must, in the words of J. Andrew Kirk, take seriously "the bias of the Christian Gospel itself ('good news to the poor . . . release to the captives . . . liberty to those who are oppressed,' Lk 4:18). . . there is no option; theology must be done from out of a commitment to a living God who defends the cause of 'the hungry' and who sends 'the rich empty away' (Lk 1:53)" (*Liberation Theology*, p. 205).

It cannot be emphasized enough that the privatization of biblical faith and subsequent Christian spirituality is a distortion. As we have seen in our earlier discussions, Yahweh is a God who cares and acts on behalf of the poor and powerless. Jesus had table-fellowship with the outcasts of his day. The history of the Church is filled with the lives of men and women who have fed the hungry, clothed the naked, visited the imprisoned, and challenged the city of man in the name of the City of God. In more recent times we have witnessed a renewed concern for the demands of social justice. The witness of Dorothy Day and Mother Teresa comes easily to mind. Thomas Merton and his book *Conjectures of a Guilty Bystander* had a profound influence on a whole generation of Christians. I remember reading this book as a college seminarian. A passage which I underlined at the time and have returned to many times reads:

> In Louisville, at the corner of 4th and Walnut, in the center of the shopping district, I was suddenly overwhelmed with the realization that I loved all those people, that they were mine and I, theirs. That we could not be alien to one another even though we were total strangers. It was like waking from a

dream of separateness, of furious self-isolation in a special world, the world of renunciation and supposed holiness. (p. 156)

Many Catholics, including the hierarchy, began to see the importance of the social dimensions of our biblical spirituality. Some of the great writings on the dignity of the human person and the sacredness of life have been penned by recent popes. For example: John XXIII's *Pacem in Terris*; Paul VI's *Populorum Progressio*; and John Paul II's *Redemptor Hominis*. The World Synod of Bishops issued a remarkable document in 1971 entitled, "Justice in the World." They wrote: "Action on behalf of justice and participation in the transformation of the world fully appear to us as a constitutive dimension of the preaching of the Gospel or, in other words, of the Church's mission for the redemption of the human race and its liberation from every oppressive situation." A faith that does justice is not a luxury or incidental to the Gospel but is at the very heart of the Church's preaching. And secondly, redemption means more than "saving souls." Redemption includes working to overcome oppressive social structures which dehumanize and disregard the image of God in which we are all wonderfully made.

Conversion, Justice, And The Church

Mary is not only a model of justice and conversion for the individual Christian, but for the Church as a whole. She says, "all generations will call me blessed." The story of God's justice (generosity) and holiness (doing the deeds of justice, mercy, strength, and right) *continues* beyond Nazareth and Jerusalem into the world and history. All generations, all people, are to esteem Mary as the one in whom God has acted in such a generous and holy way. The life of Mary speaks to the life of the Church in a timeless and timely fashion. Such a relationship was not lost on the early Church's theologians, pastors, and saints.

Irenaeus understood Mary's Magnificat to be a song of prophecy. Mary is the Church to come, fulfilling the promise to Abraham. Redemption has come through the Word made flesh in Mary. Irenaeus wrote:

> Who else reigns in the house of Jacob for ever, but Christ Jesus our Lord, Son of the most High? He gave His promise in the Law and the Prophets, that He would make manifest His salvation to all flesh: for this He became a Son of Man, that man might become a Son of God. Therefore Mary rejoiced, and speaking prophetically in the Church's name, said, 'My soul doth magnify the Lord.' All is renewed, when the Word newly made flesh begins the task of winning back to God mankind who had strayed so far from God. (*Against Heresies* 3:10:2)

St. Ambrose relates Mary's singing of the Magnificat to the Church's proclamation of the Gospel through history: "Watch Mary, my children, for the word prophetically uttered of the Church, applies to her also: 'How lovely thy sandalled steps, O princely maid!' Yes, princely and lovely indeed are the Church's steps, as she goes to announce her Gospel of joy: lovely the steps of Mary and the Church."

And our final example is supplied by St. Cyril of Alexandria in a sermon delivered in 431 at the Council of Ephesus: "And so, brethren, may it be granted to us to adore with deep humility the indivisible Trinity. And then let us praise with songs of joy Mary ever virgin, who herself is clearly the holy Church, together with her Son and most chaste spouse. To God be praise forever."

The life, ministry, and hope of glory revealed in Mary is also that of the Church. The Church is called to incarnate the poor flesh

of the Word in her everyday life and ministry. She must be in
solidarity with the poor, the lowly, the powerless, and the oppressed wherever and whenever they cry for justice and liberation.
And the Church is a messianic community which lives by hope in
the One who is our hope. The Church is in need of constant reform
and forgiveness. She is never above the message she preaches but
also waits for the Lord to return in full glory. Until that time the
Church waits in patient hope for His return.

The Church is just to the extent that she *does* justice within her
own community. Her words alone cannot be bold. Words of justice
demand deeds of justice. Our own community must be one of
liberation, generosity, holiness, and love. We cannot claim to
know God if we fail at justice. The prophet Jeremiah preaches:

> Do you think you are a king because you compete in cedar?
> Did not your father eat and drink and do justice and righteous-
> ness? Then it was well with him. He judged the cause of the
> poor and needy; then it was well. Is not this to know me? says
> the Lord. (Jr 22:15-16)

The king and the priest (the leaders of the community) cannot
claim to know God in spirit and truth if the requirements of justice
are ignored. Piety without the deeds of justice is offensive. The
prophet Micah:

> "With what shall I come before the Lord, and bow myself
> before the God on high? Shall I come before him with burnt
> offerings, with calves a year old? Will the Lord be pleased with
> offerings of rams, with ten thousands of rivers of oil? Shall I
> give my first born for my transgression, the fruit of my body
> for the sin of my soul?" He has shown you, O man, what is
> good; and what does the Lord require of you but to do justice,
> and to love kindness, and to walk humbly with your God?
> (Mi 6:6-8)

The words of Jesus continue the prophets' preaching for justice within the community of the covenant. The prophets in the Old Testament often preached against those who tried to neutralize the demands of justice by retreating into cultic worship. The effect was most devastating: both justice and liturgy became perverted. Jesus confronts the religious authorities of His day who take refuge in the formal observance of the Law. The Law and the promise of the covenant have become badges of privilege and superiority. However, the authentic purpose of the Law — to know God and do His will through deeds of justice and mercy — has been forgotten. The words of Jesus: "Woe to you, scribes and Pharisees, hypocrites, because you tithe the mint and the dill and the cummin and neglect the more important parts of the Law: justice and mercy and loyalty" (Mt 23:23).

The Magnificat of Mary is a song of praise for what God has done in justice (generosity), holiness (deeds of generosity), and mercy. God is praised by Mary and all generations because He is attentive to the poor and the outcast. The Church continues throughout history to be the concrete, ever present, reminder of God's love for the poor and the oppressed. In the Fourth Gospel Jesus prays the following words to his Father: "I do not pray that you should take them out of the world, but that you should keep them from the evil one" (Jn 17:15). The Christian community is not to retreat from the great issues of the day. The Church cannot remain indifferent or "so heavenly" that the cries of the oppressed and the poor are ignored. Lazarus is still outside the door with only the dogs to lick his sores. The Christian community remains in the world as a prophetic voice calling *itself* and nations to do justice. The Church must avoid becoming domesticated by the worldly powers of privilege and might. The evil one continues to tempt the Church to side with the rich and the oppressors. However, the Church, "the little flock" formed by the One who became our poor flesh, is on the side of the victims of history and not its worldly victors. The temptation to side with the powerful is not new. We need only consider the words contained in the Letter of James:

> My brethren, show no partiality as you hold the faith of our Lord Jesus Christ, the Lord of glory. For if a man with gold rings and in fine clothing comes into your assembly, and a poor man in shabby clothing also comes in, and you pay attention to the one who wears the fine clothing and say, "Have a seat here, please," while you say to the poor man, "Stand there" or "Sit at my feet," have you not made distinctions among yourselves, and become judges with evil thoughts? Listen, my beloved brethren. Has not God chosen those who are poor in the world to be rich in faith and heirs of the kingdom He has promised to those who love Him? But you have dishonored the poor man. Is it not the rich who oppress you, is it not they who drag you into court? Is it not they who blaspheme the honorable name which was invoked over you? (Jm 2:1-7)

Church Of The Poor

The noted liberation theologian Jon Sobrino, S.J. in his latest book, *The True Church And The Poor*, makes a very telling distinction: a true justice Church must not only be *for* the poor but *of* the poor. Mary would certainly have understood and appreciated this distinction. She identifies herself as one of the Anawim — "The Poor Ones" of Yahweh — since she is a woman, poor, and a lowly virgin. Mary is poor not only in spirit but in her physical resources. This is crucial for the Church. The message of the Kingdom of God, entrusted to the Church, is never about merely giving to the poor so as to turn them into objects of welfare or charity. On the contrary. It is the poor who are essential to the Church being the Church. In the words of Father Sobrino: "the poor evangelize the Church." What he means by this is quite profound: the Church does not possess God and saving knowledge (*gnosis*); rather the true Church is possessed by the Spirit and continues the saving *action* of Jesus. The emphasis of the Church *of* the poor is on *action* — doing God's liberating will. "The theological concern is not to explain as accurately as possible what the essence of sin is, or what meaning a sinful world has, or what meaning human existence has in such a world. The concern is to change the sinful situation."

There is not only the temptation of the Church to be a Church of the victors and the powerful, but there is also the temptation to reduce the Gospel to some humanitarian program or economic plan of redistribution, or to identify it with a specific political ideology (Marxism or capitalism). This temptation must be rejected as vigorously as the temptation to sit with the mighty. The words of Mary can serve as an important reminder: ". . . for He who is mighty has done great things for me . . ." The Church brings the good news of what God *has* done, and what God *continues* to do, and what God *will* do in the future. Without the centrality of the Kingdom of God our doing justice too easily becomes a form of self-righteousness, arrogance, and eventually fanaticism. Without the Kingdom of God as the ultimate critique of *all* political and economic systems, it becomes easy to elevate one system or program to ultimacy. The result is idolatry with its eventual repression, violence, and death. Too often we have witnessed the changing of one set of oppressors for another set. The faces change but the game is the same.

The testimonies of the Bible and history teach us a very fundamental and humbling lesson: all have sinned; all have fallen short of the glory of God; and all are in need of conversion and healing. Virtue is not the exclusive claim of those on the right or the left; conservative or liberal; Marxist or capitalist. The Christian brings to working for social justice this "realism" about the human condition and the need for God's action and Kingdom. The Christian community is more than another political action group or social welfare agency. It proclaims by word and deed the *justice of God*. Father Francis X. Meehan captures the difference justice done in the name of Yahweh-Jesus brings:

> . . . a caution is desperately needed. "Social justice" is a term that non-Christians also use. Church people, as Pope John Paul II seems to be saying, must always have another dimension to their justice. . . We must, as Christians, learn to do these things with a *difference*. Justice, in the New Testament, always carries the memory of God's justice. And God's justice is more than merely ethical. It is a justice that itself justifies through the God-given gifts of love and reconciliation. . . We must look into the eyes of the enemy, of the oppressor, of the general, of the corporate executive, and see there the spark of God. (*A Contemporary Social Spirituality*, pp. 121-122)

These words of Father Meehan highlight the real difference between a worldly liberation and the authentic liberation of the Kingdom. The difference lies in *Reconciliation*. The Christian, under the guidance of the Spirit, seeks to turn the enemy into a friend and works to overcome evil and violence through grace and forgiveness. None of this is to suggest that we seek a cheap peace and overlook real injustices in order to get along. But authentic justice and liberation has as its goal a reconciliation which allows all people to walk together. We never become so righteous and the enemy so evil as to deny the possibility of error by the righteous and goodness in the enemy. The words of the Crucified Jesus ground all Christian justice: ''Father, forgive them for they know not what they do'' (Lk 23:34).

CHAPTER

3

Mercy And Justice

"And His mercy is on those who fear Him from generation to generation." (Lk 1:50)

Mary continues her litany of praise concerning the attributes of God. In verse fifty God's mercy takes center stage. We cannot help but feel a little confused about this little verse which contains a great deal of spiritual nourishment. Mary proclaims the mercy of God as it comes to those who fear Him. Mercy and fear, at first blush, just don't seem to go together. We have trouble fitting the two concepts into an harmonious pattern. However, Mary had no such difficulty. In order to help relieve some of our uneasiness, it will be essential to uncover the biblical meaning of these words. Secondly, we will need to relate these words — mercy and fear — to Mary. Thirdly, an important issue for our study will be the relationship between mercy and justice. And finally, we need to examine the relationship between mercy and justice for our individual Christian witness and that of the Church. Once again the Magnificat indicates that God's mercy extends into history (generation to generation).

Mercy

The word "mercy" has a rich biblical pedigree. While there is no truly satisfactory translation of the Hebrew word *hesed*, scholars most often associate it with mercy. *Hesed* or mercy is one of the foundational experiences of Hebrew religion and morality. As with our discussion of holiness (see Chapter Two) we cannot define mercy with "clear and distinct" Cartesian definitions but we must understand it in descriptive terms. We know what mercy is by the way mercy is experienced. God's mercy and the mercy expected from those who live the covenant become clear as we highlight the various experiences associated with mercy.

Biblical scholars tell us that the word *hesed* or mercy is experienced in five specific ways in the Old Testament (See John L. McKenzie, S.J., *Dictionary of the Bible*, "Mercy"):

1. *FIDELITY* (*emet*). The mercy of God is first and foremost experienced by fidelity. God is faithful to His promises. Unlike the human heart which is fickle, easily distracted, and caught up in the latest fad, God's mercy endures for all eternity. God's fidelity is never determined by the infidelity of His people. They may be, and often are, unfaithful but God continues to keep His word. Time and again God continues to call Israel back to the covenant. God is a tenacious lover who will simply not give up on His people. The effects of God's mercy or *hesed* are quite profound. God's faithful mercy empowers us to be faithful in dealing with one another and with God. The people of the covenant are faithful and merciful *because* God has shown the way. Also there is a cumulative effect — faithful mercy breeds faithful mercy. The following verses from Proverbs help to highlight the effects of mercy: "A man who is kind benefits himself, but a cruel man hurts himself. A wicked man earns deceptive wages, but one who sows righteousness gets a sure reward" (Pr 11:17-18); "He who despises his neighbor is a sinner, but happy is he who is kind to the poor. Do they not err that devise evil? Those who devise good meet loyalty and faithfulness"

(Pr 14:21-22); and ''What is desired in a man is loyalty, and a poor man is better than a liar. The fear of the Lord leads to life; and he who has it rests satisfied; he will not be visited by harm'' (Pr 19:22-23). Mercy is above all faithful when the one (the poor man) to whom mercy and kindness are shown cannot return the kindness. This is where God's *hesed* comes into play. For God's mercy will be extended to those who are merciful. In the words of the Beatitudes: ''Blessed are the merciful, for they shall obtain mercy'' (Mt 5:7).

2. *JUDGMENT (mispat)*. God's mercy is also associated with judgment. From the perspective of the Hebrew Bible the word ''judgment'' *(mispat)* is associated with the experience of God's righteousness and justice. Mercy is intimately related to justice since the biblical experience of justice is generosity (see Chapter One and the discussion of justice as generosity). There is a special command placed on the powerful to show mercy to the weak and the poor. This special command is very important for the king or the ruler of a nation. The political leader cannot be concerned only with a rising GNP or military security. There is a profound *moral* dimension to political authority. The king, if he is to resemble the King of Kings, must be a leader in justice and generosity. The poor, weak, lowly, and voiceless must find a hearing in the court of the powerful. God is the King who ''works justice for all who are oppressed'' (Ps 103:6). The kingly reign of God is one that is generous to all the peoples of the earth. The prophet Jeremiah puts it as follows:

> Thus says the Lord: "Let not the wise man glory in his wisdom, let not the mighty man glory in his might, let not the rich man glory in his riches; but let him who glories glory in this, that he understands and knows me, that I am the Lord who practices steadfast love, justice, and righteousness in the earth; for in these things I delight, says the Lord." (Jr 9:23-24).

The king, the political leader, the person of means and intelligence have all been given abundant blessings from the God of generosity and mercy. Hence, to whom much is given much is expected. Those who have received much must also share with those in need. The power of the powerful is to exhibit the mercy of the God of all mercies.

3. *RIGHTEOUSNESS* (*sedakah*). The attribute of judgment is closely related to righteousness which naturally relates both terms to justice. God's justice (His generosity) is merciful because it demands that those in authority use their power to help the lowly and oppressed. Those in authority are under God's just judgment. Those in power must exercise their power in a spirit of righteousness. This righteousness is grounded in God's action of *deliverance* and rescuing the poor. The righteousness of God, and the corresponding duty of the powerful to be righteous, is expressed in many of the Psalms:

> O continue Thy steadfast love to those who know Thee,
> and Thy salvation to the upright of heart!
> Let not the foot of arrogance come upon me,
> nor the hand of the wicked drive me away.
> There the evildoers lie prostrate,
> they are thrust down, unable to rise. (Ps 36:10-12)

Psalm 40 looks with expectation to the Lord whose love is faithful and protective. God does not abandon His people:

> Do not Thou, O Lord, withhold Thy mercy from me,
> let Thy steadfast love and Thy faithfulness ever preserve me!
>
> Be pleased, O Lord, to deliver me!
> O Lord make haste to help me!
> Let them be put to shame and confusion
> altogether who seek to snatch my life; . . .

But may all who seek Thee rejoice and be glad in Thee;
may those who love Thy salvation say continually,
"Great is the Lord!" (Ps 40:11, 13, 16)

And our final example comes by way of Psalm 143. This is a royal or kingly Psalm which implores the Lord to act so His people and their leaders may live free from the harm of enemies:

Deliver me, O Lord, from my enemies!
I have fled to Thee for refuge!
Teach me to do Thy will, for Thou art my God!
Let Thy good spirit lead me on a level path!
For Thy name's sake, O Lord, preserve my life!
In Thy righteousness bring me out of trouble!
And in Thy steadfast love cut off my enemies,
and destroy all my adversaries,
for I am Thy servant. (Ps 143:9-12)

4. *SALVATION* (*yesua*). One of the most powerful expressions of Yahweh's mercy is in His actions on behalf of salvation or liberation. Yahweh is a God Who saves. Of course the great example of Yahweh's mighty deed of salvation is the Exodus. God will not allow His people to perish. There is also a tender aspect to His mercy experienced as salvation. The prophets draw heavily on the imagery of marriage to explain the love between Yahweh and Israel. God's love and mercy are protective as a father watches over his family. Yahweh can never remain indifferent to the suffering and misfortune of His bride Israel. He has a deep *pathos* or feeling for Israel that no amount of waywardness can destroy. The prophet Jeremiah writes:

The word of the Lord came to me, saying, "Go and proclaim in the hearing of Jerusalem, Thus says the Lord, 'I remember the devotion of your youth, your love as a bride, how you followed Me in the wilderness, in a land not sown.' " (Jr 2:1-2)

Yahweh's mercy and love are restorative. Even in a distant land Yahweh will not forget Israel:

Thus says the Lord: "The people who survived the sword found grace in the wilderness; when Israel sought for rest, the Lord appeared to him from afar. I have loved you with an everlasting love; therefore I have continued My faithfulness to you. Again I will build you, and you shall be built, O virgin Israel!" (Jr 31:2-4)

Every wise parent knows that love requires patience and does not make demands that only frustrate and embitter. Yahweh is a wise parent Who does not forget the limitations of the human condition:

For as the heavens are high above the earth, so great is His steadfast love towards those who fear Him; as far as the east is from the west, so far does He remove our transgressions from us. As a father pities his children, so the Lord pities those who fear Him. For He knows our frame; He remembers that we are dust. (Ps 103:11-13)

5. *COVENANT* (*berit*). God's mercy, generosity, and justice place requirements on Israel. Israel must be a nation which mirrors God's holiness and justice and righteousness. This is essential to the covenant or relationship. As Yahweh has done for Israel so the members of the community must do for one another. Israel cannot do as she pleases or play fast and loose with God's love. When she breaks the covenant, especially through idolatry and social injustice, Yahweh shows the folly of such infidelity. In the book of Exodus we read:

"You shall not make for yourself a graven image, or any likeness of anything that is in heaven above, or that is in the earth beneath, or that is in the water under the earth; you shall not bow down to them or serve them; for I the Lord your God am a jealous God, visiting the iniquity of the fathers upon the children to the third and the fourth generation of those who hate Me, but showing steadfast love to thousands of those who love Me and keep My commandments." (Ex 20:4-6)

The above quoted passage from Exodus reminds us that while God's anger will extend to future generations (the third and fourth), the steadfast love of God is far greater. Obedience to the covenant brings mercy to untold numbers. Mary clearly echoes this idea in her testimony to God's mercy ''from generation to generation.''

A word of caution should be raised: God's fidelity and mercy as expressed in the covenant do *NOT* depend on Israel's fidelity. In fact we know that often Israel is less than faithful. Yet Yahweh remains faithful through the power of His forgiving love. The book of Numbers recounts the prayer of Moses as he appeals to Yahweh's greatness as a Forgiving Lover:

And now, I pray Thee, let the power of the Lord be great as Thou hast promised '. . .Pardon the iniquity of this people, I pray Thee, according to the greatness of Thy steadfast love, and according as Thou had forgiven this people, from Egypt even until now.' (Nb 14:17, 19)

Notice that Moses appeals to the saving action of God in the past. Yahweh acted in a mighty way to liberate His people from the bondage of Egypt. The liberation was not because the Hebrews merited such deliverance. The sole motivation for the Exodus was God's gracious love. And now, even though Israel has fallen into idolatry and infidelity, Moses still calls upon God for deliverance and mercy.

The New Testament also has some important insights about mercy (*eleos*). Mercy is most powerfully expressed in the ministry of Jesus, especially through table-fellowship with the sinner, the outcast, and the wretched of his day. The Pharisees and the other respectable folk were very troubled by Jesus' eating and associating with sinners. There can be no mercy without the willingness to forgive. And there can be no genuine forgiveness without the willingness to make human contact with the one who needs forgiveness. Isn't this the very message of the Incarnation? God became our poor flesh because we needed to be forgiven and accepted by the One who is Unconditional Acceptance. Could God have stayed in heaven and healed at a distance? God can do what He wills. However, God emptying Himself of glory, and becoming one with our poor condition, indicates that there can be no real reconciliation without sacrifice and the willingness to let go of power, glory, and privilege. God's mercy in the Incarnation gives us an example: as God has been merciful to us, as God has forgiven us in Jesus, we are to show mercy and forgiveness to one another. Jesus' words are very telling: "Woe to you, scribes and Pharisees, hypocrites! For you tithe the mint and the dill and the cummin and have neglected the weighty matters of the law, justice and mercy and faith; these you ought to have done, without neglecting the others. You blind guides, straining out a gnat and swallowing a camel!" (Mt 23:23-24).

Both the Hebrew Scriptures and the New Testament agree that mercy is an activity as well as a sentiment (*pathos*). If mercy remains only a feeling, then it easily becomes romantic and ineffective. If mercy is only good works without the recognition of God having first shown us mercy, then it easily becomes a source of boasting or pride. The Letter of James clearly indicates that *both* faith and works, mercy and good deeds are necessary: "What does it profit, my brethren, if a man says he has faith but has not works? Can his faith save him? If a brother or sister is ill-clad and in lack of daily food, and one of you says to them, 'Go in peace, be warmed and filled,' without giving them the things needed for the body, what does it profit? So faith by itself, if it has no works, is dead'' (Jm 2:14-17).

Fear

The Magnificat of Mary indicates that God's mercy comes to those who fear Him. Does this mean that we must first fear God, in the sense of trembling before Him because of His wrath, before we can experience His mercy? Must we be scared before we can be saved? Unfortunately there is much in our religious past which would seem to say ''yes.'' Too often we have been presented as ''sinners in the hands of an angry God.'' The God of the fiery mountain (Sinai) must be appeased. We must jump through the hoops and please this divine Judge or Bookkeeper Who knows all our sins and never forgets. Fear first; then mercy will follow.

This is not the Lord and God proclaimed by Mary. Yet the question persists: Why the mention of fear? In order to answer this question and gain insight into why Mary can attest to God's mercy on those who fear Him, it will be necessary to understand what the Bible means by ''fear of the Lord.'' Rabbi Abraham Joshua Heschel, the great teacher and religious leader of this century, will be our guide for appreciating ''fear of the Lord.''

Rabbi Heschel teaches that all reality has about it a sublime dimension; a rumor of angels (Peter Berger); a hint of the transcendent. When we become aware of this divine dimension of existence we move into wonder. Wonder is an attitude which moves us to question the gift of life and all that surrounds us. We come to realize that all that is comes from a power beyond our willing and doing. There is about existence a profound gratuitous aspect. We realize that life and others are precious. Before these gratuitous and wondrous aspects of existence we must give thanks.

Wonder is the beginning of faith. Yet there is another dimension — a maturing aspect to wonder. Heschel indicates that wonder can pass into *awe*. *Awe* and *fear* come from the same Hebrew word *yirah*. However, there is an important distinction between awe and fear. Rabbi Heschel writes:

> Fear is the anticipation and expectation of evil or pain, as contrasted with hope which is the anticipation of good. Awe, on the other hand, is the sense of wonder and humility inspired by the sublime or felt in the presence of mystery. . . Awe, unlike fear, does not make us shrink from the awe-inspiring object, but, on the contrary, draws us near to it. This is why awe is compatible with both love and joy. In a sense, awe is the antithesis of fear. To feel "The Lord is my light and my salvation" is to feel "Whom shall I fear?" (Ps 27:1) (*God in Search of Man*, p. 77)

If we draw on the distinction between fear and awe supplied by Heschel we can say that God's mercy is upon those who are in awe of His many benefits. And true awe, the kind of awe possessed by Mary, is for those who are in awe because God is God. There is a profound sense of humility and unworthiness in the presence of God. Yet there is no feeling of self-hatred or self-rejection. In the presence of God we come to experience a true (humble) sense of our condition and just how much God has bestowed on us in mercy and generosity (justice). In God's presence we experience love and joy. The lowliness of Mary's condition (poor, female, and virginal) does not prevent her from recognizing how blessed she is throughout the generations. In fact, it is because she knows she is poor and needful that Mary is a woman of great wisdom. Rabbi Heschel:

> The beginning of awe is wonder, and the beginning of wisdom is awe. . . The foundations of the world are not of this world. . . Ultimate meaning and ultimate wisdom are not found within the world but in God, and the only way to wisdom is . . .

through our relationship to God. That relationship is *awe*. (*God in Search of Man*)

Mary: Mercy And Awe

Theologian John C. Merkle in his outstanding study of the depth theology of Abraham Joshua Heschel, *The Genesis of Faith*, makes the distinction between the will to wonder (way of wonder) and the will to power (way of expediency). The will to wonder takes no one and nothing for granted. All reality is appreciated and is reflective of God's goodness, mercy, and generosity. The way of wonder allows us to relate to the world in order to respond and not control. The way of wonder leads to the way of appreciation. We do not use others or the world but allow them to reveal themselves as they are. Heschel says it powerfully: "Mankind will not perish for want of information; but only from want of appreciation. The beginning of our happiness lies in the understanding that life without wonder is not worth living" (*Man is not Alone*, p. 37).

In contrast to the will to wonder and the way of appreciation is the will to power and the way of expediency. Power and expediency (we will have more to say about this in our next chapter) evidence themselves in deeds of exploitation and looking out for number one. Everything that is done must be done with an eye to our advantage or self-interest. The will to power stirs our drive to manipulate others and the world around us. The philosopher Martin Heidegger terms this orientation toward reality as "standing reserve." That is, all things, including people, are looked upon as resources to be used, managed, and organized for our goals. There is no fellowship or reverence, just opportunities to exploit.

The Magnificat of Mary clearly expresses her being-in-the-world as a woman of wonder and awe; the way of appreciation rather than the way of exploitation and the will to power. Mary is constantly aware that He who is mighty has done great things for her. This awareness (mindfulness) that the Almighty has been merciful moves Mary to a profound sense of indebtedness and praise. She knows that all she owns she owes. She is not sufficient unto herself. Mary is gifted. But this giftedness is never a cause for arrogance but of gratitude and praise.

Rabbi Heschel makes a telling point about indebtedness: When we realize that we have been graced by God, we also come to realize that we are obligated to *respond*. God asks something of us and waits for a response. God asks each of us: What are you to live for? The ego offers an easy answer: We live for ourselves and our projects. The pride-filled ego proclaims its own agenda and works and pomps. The ego goes the way of the will to power and control. Everything and everyone is to be exploited for one's own needs and demands.

By contrast, the way of indebtedness challenges the arrogance and hard-heartedness of the ego. The way of indebtedness speaks to us of the need to do God's will. This takes the heavy burden off our shoulders and frees us from the illusions and burdens of self-sufficiency. We are what is not ours. Rabbi Heschel:

All that is left to us is a choice — to answer or to refuse to answer. Yet the more deeply we listen, the more we become stripped of the arrogance and callousness which alone would enable us to refuse. We carry a load of marvel, wishing to exchange it for the simplicity of knowing what to live for, a load which we can never lay down nor continue to carry not knowing where.

If awe is rare, if wonder is dead, and the sense of mystery defunct, then the problem what to do with awe, wonder and mystery does not exist, and one does not sense being asked. The awareness of being asked is easily repressed, for it is an echo of the intimation that is small and still. It will not, however, remain forever subdued. The day comes when the still small intimation becomes "like the wind and storm, fulfilling His word." (*Who Is Man?*, pp. 110-111)

The will to power and the way of exploitation are constantly trying to keep our sense of awe and indebtedness beyond consciousness. Yet grace and mercy does penetrate our hearts of stone and eyes shut with pride. We say, "I am because I am *called upon* to be."

Mercy, Awe, And Justice

To be aware that we are not our own; that we are called on by another beyond ourselves; that we have been graced; and that the Almighty has done great things for us is to be indebted. This indebtedness begins in our hearts but must not remain there. From him to whom much is given much is expected. Indebtedness evokes a sense of being *required*. Naturally this causes problems for the modern mind. We understand love (like forgiveness) as something which never says it's sorry or makes demands on anyone about anything. The modern mind shudders when confronted with requirements or demands. All of this sounds like a loss of freedom and the attaching of strings. Yet biblical faith counsels another way: we are indebted and we are required to share in the work of God for others. We must continue the work of justice because we have been (and *continue* to be) on the receiving end of God's generous love. To be on the receiving end is also to be on the giving end. What goes around must come around.

The God whom Mary calls Lord and Savior is the God who cares for the poor and the oppressed. The forgotten truth of the human condition is this: We are all poor and oppressed. We are all powerless and in need of grace. The illusion is to live as if we were master and lord. Mary, the lowly, poor virgin, is aware of being blessed and of being indebted. She has a role to play and suffering-love to endure. This is costly grace. Rabbi Heschel goes so far as to say that essential to being human is the ability of being required and *responding* (response-able):

> What is involved in authentic living is not only an intuition of meaning but sensitivity to demand, not a purpose but an expectation. Sensitivity to demands is as inherent in being human as physiological functions are in human beings. . . To the Greek mind, man is above all a rational being; rationality makes him compatible with the cosmos. To the biblical mind, man is above all a commanded being, a being on whom demands may be made. The central problem is not: What is being? But rather: What is required of me? (*Who Is Man?*, pp. 106-107)

Hence each persons has demands placed upon him or her. These demands touch on the very heart of what it means *to be* human. God challenges each of us to transcend ourselves and go beyond the demands of the private-self and the ego's will to power. God's care for the poor and the powerless must be a caring that is shared and required of us. By doing justice to the poor and ministering to the anguished cry of the oppressed, we show love and gratitude to God. Mary's life is a beautiful example of indebtedness and requiredness. One example will suffice: after the Annunciation by the angel Gabriel, Mary goes *in haste* to be with Elizabeth. Elizabeth is in need of someone to share her joy and her burdens. Mary, the mother of the Lord, will respond. And the baby in Elizabeth's womb jumps for joy!

The Church Of Justice And Mercy

There is about indebtedness and requiredness a community dimension. Personal holiness is necessary but never sufficient. Social structures or communities which seek justice are necessary but never sufficient. We need individuals and communities who hunger for justice and let mercy flow daily. The Church of Jesus the incarnate Word, the community which draws inspiration from Mary, must stand in solidarity with those who know only the cruelty that comes to those who live without power in a world that idolizes power. The Church must be *for* the poor and a Church *of* the poor. Only by being one with and for and of the poor can we as a faith community echo Mary's words: "My soul magnifies the Lord. . . He Who is mighty has done great things for me (us),. . . And His mercy is on those who fear Him."

The Second Vatican Council made a serious effort to be a Church of the poor and a Church that is poor. What occasioned this new sensitivity to the wretched of the earth? Father Karl Rahner, S.J.'s analysis of the theological significance of the Council is most insightful. He advances the thesis that for the first time in the Church's history it discovered itself as a *WORLD-CHURCH*. The history of the Church can be divided into three great epochs: the brief period of Judaeo-Christianity; the Church that wedded itself to Hellenism and European culture and civilization; and the third epoch, the one we find with the Second Vatican Council, in which the Church is now a World-Church. Father Rahner writes:

> What we are saying is that the Second Vatican Council is the beginning of a tentative approach by the Church to the discovery and official realization of itself as *World-Church*. This thesis may seem exaggerated and it certainly needs to be explained much more precisely before it can be made to sound acceptable. It is of course also misleading if only because the Church was always *in potentia* World-Church and because the actualizing of this potentiality itself involved a long histori- cal process of coming-to-be, the origins of which coincides with the beginning of European colonialism and of the mod- ern world-mission of the Church from the sixteenth century, an actualizing which is not completely finished even today. But if we look at the macroscopic and official acting of

> the Church and at the same time become more clearly aware
> that the concrete, real activity of the Church . . . was what we
> might venture to describe as that of an export firm, exporting
> to the whole world a European religion along with other
> elements of this supposedly superior culture and civilization,
> and not really attempting to change the commodity, then it
> seems appropriate and justified to regard Vatican II as the first
> great official event in which the Church came to be realized as
> *World-Church*. ("Basic Theological Interpretation of the
> Second Vatican Council," *Concern for the Church*. Theolog-
> ical Investigations XX, p. 78)

The World-Church of which Rahner speaks is one in which
the voices of concern; the agenda for discussion; the theologizing;
and the understanding of what it means to be Church are no longer
of one color, culture, or civilization. The World-Church is like the
many-colored coat of Joseph. The World-Church is one which
speaks from the experiences of the Asians, Africans, and Latins.
This World-Church ushers in not merely quantitative change but a
qualitative one. The cries of the poor, the oppressed, the exploited,
and the powerless are now front and center. The transmission of
Christianity from Judaeo-Christianity to Gentile Christianity has
moved to a Christianity of Liberation on behalf of all who are
oppressed. Christianity is not to be counted with the victors but the
victims; not those who write history but the poor of history who will
help usher in the Kingdom of God. The bishops from Asia, Africa,
and Latin America at Vatican II brought with them an agenda
which ushered in a new epoch. Dominican theologian Marie-
Dominique Chenu, O.P. has written:

> More and more, during the two last sessions of the Council,
> and especially with the production of the second Constitution
> on the Church in the World of Today, there came to be
> increasingly active participation by the bishops of the poor

nations, of the Third World, as it is called, working both to reinforce that mystical vision and to spell out the practical demands that follow from it. In Fall a greater and more lucid solidarity gradually grew up between the bishops of rich industrialized areas and those of the developing countries. The appalling problem of the economic and political development of the world was thus reflected as a living image in the Church itself: this new awareness could only intensify the harsh words of the Gospel. ("Vatican II and the Church of the Poor," *The Poor and the Church*, edited by Norbert Greinacher and Alois Miller. Concilium. Religion in the Seventies. Vol. 104, p. 60)

This new awareness of the harsh words of the Gospel is not a call to be angry or self-righteous. It is an invitation to proclaim the greatness of God's justice and mercy from generation to generation. How? By being individuals and communities which follow the example of Mary — the poor virgin who let God's will be done in and through her. The Word became poor flesh and became one with our poor flesh. God's will must *continue* through history as, in the name of justice, we do mercy: we feed the hungry, clothe the naked, visit the sick, speak for the voiceless, provide shelter for the homeless, extend the oil of gladness and the kiss of peace to those who are undeserving but needful, and above all, announce the year of the Lord's favor and His liberation to those in bondage.

CHAPTER

4

Power And Justice

"He has shown strength with His arm, He has scattered the
proud in the imagination of their hearts, He has put down
the mighty from their thrones, and exalted those of low
degree; He has filled the hungry with good things, and the
rich He has sent empty away." (Lk 1:51-53)

A major theme that is predominant throughout the Gospel of
Luke is what biblical scholar Allen Vershey calls "the great reversal." Throughout the Gospel there is a transformation and reversal
of what is expected. The Jesus who preaches the Kingdom of God
in Luke is one who confounds the values and beliefs of the Jewish
religion, Greek philosophy, and a kind of naturalism which judges
by surface appearances. Jesus constantly challenges His audience
(and of course this includes the modern audience) to go beyond the
conventional wisdom, the taken for granted faith of the less than
faithful, and the daily cynicism of the jaded fold who have seen it
all, heard it all, and experienced it all. Jesus invites His audience to
be open to God's surprises and the working of the Spirit.

Another biblical and literary scholar, John Dominic Crossan

has written extensively on the parables of Jesus as stories about God's activity of reversing human expectations. In his fascinating little book, *The Dark Interval*, Professor Crossan contrasts the parables of Jesus with the myths of the Pharisees and the smug. Myths are in the business of world-building. Myths explain the world for us and provide security and a sense of meaning. Myths are necessary for individual and group life and growth. Without myths we fall victim to anomie and instead of living we merely exist (suicide is high for individuals and groups without a major myth or story). However, there is a danger that our myths become idols and ends in themselves. We come to worship the story rather than the deeper reality to which the myth points. Anything which challenges our myths becomes a threat and must be silenced by ridicule or even violence and death. Myths come to resist change.

Professor Crossan makes the point that a number of Jesus' parables are told with an eye to challenging myths become idols. Parables are told which subvert the major stories of the day which claim to know with absolute certainty what is good, true, and beautiful. The parables of reversal challenge the too secure and self-righteous world of the morally self-superior who look down in judgment upon others. Constantly Jesus confronts those whose moral and spiritual world leave no room for surprises, conversion, and above all God's saving grace. Parables make room in our myths (our prevailing stories) for God to do His thing. Parables aim at getting us to loosen up our thinking so a new, more inclusive, God-active world can come into being. W.H. Auden in "For The Time Being," put it this way:

> Therefore, see without looking, hear without listening, breathe without asking: The Inevitable is what will seem to happen to you purely by chance; The Real is what will strike you as really absurd; Unless you are certain you are dreaming, it is certainly a dream of your own; Unless you exclaim — "There must be some mistake" — you must be mistaken.

Myths make no room for ''There must be some mistake'' while parables thrive on the absurd, the shocking, and those things which confound human reason.

The Gospel of Luke contains a number of parables of reversal which challenge the too comfortable and near world that has been built by myths. Professor Crossan, in his book *In Parables*, highlights six such parables of reversal in Luke: the Good Samaritan (Lk 10:30-37); the Rich Man and Lazarus (Lk 16:19-31); the Pharisee and the Publican (Lk 18:10-14); the Wedding Guests who claim the first seats of honor only to have their positions reversed with those who sit in the lower places (Lk 14:1-24); The Great Supper in which the invited do *not* come and the uninvited are the true banqueters (Lk 15:11-32); the Prodigal Son (Lk 15:11-32). Each of these six parables announce the Kingdom's challenge to the too narrow world of truth and goodness built by myth. Professor Crossan provides the following helpful schema:

GOOD	BAD
1. Priest and Levites	Samaritan
2. Rich Man	Lazarus
3. Pharisee	Publican
4. First-seated	Last-seated
5. Invited Guests	Uninvited Guests
6. Dutiful Son	Prodigal Son

Not only does Jesus *tell* parables but Jesus is himself the *Parable of God*, for the birth, passion, death and resurrection of Jesus confound the proud and shake the mighty from their thrones. Consider the following: The Ancient One who lives in unapproachable light has become poor flesh like us (Jn 1:14). The suffering, rejected, and worldly powerless Jesus challenges all the popular expectations and job-descriptions for the Messiah. No self-respecting Messiah would allow himself to die on a cross. And finally, our well thought out philosophy does not admit of the dead coming back to life. The words of Paul to the cultured and religious people at Corinth powerfully capture how the teller of parables has become the very Parable of God:

> For the word of the cross is folly to those who are perishing, but to us who are being saved it is the power of God. For it is written, "I will destroy the wisdom of the wise, and the cleverness of the clever I will thwart." Where is the wise man? Where is the scribe? Where is the debater of this age? Has not God made foolish the wisdom of the world?. . . For Jews demand signs and Greeks seek wisdom, but we preach Christ crucified. . . For the foolishness of God is wiser than men, and the weakness of God is stronger than men. (I Cor 1:18-20; 22, 25)

The Magnificat as a whole, and especially the three verses which introduce this chapter, proclaims the wisdom of God and the surprising ways of His grace. The proud are brought low and the humble are exalted; the mighty no longer enjoy their privileged positions and the lowly are now established with dignity. Those who are in need are filled with the good gifts of a loving Father while the rich of this world go the way of their riches where glory quickly passes. Mary is hailed as full of grace because she is open to the surprises of God's Word which has become enfleshed in her. Mary is a servant and handmaid of the Lord because she does not try to limit God's actions by appeals to existing religious expectations, philosophy, or the hard-headed common sense which cynically views the wonders of God. This does not mean that Mary is not questioning and troubled. She is. Mary wants to know how she is going to conceive without sexual intercourse. Her question is motivated by awe and wonder and not idle curiosity. Because she trusts God, He who is mighty is able to do great things for her and through her. The lowly, poor, and uncelebrated virgin will be counted among the low who are exalted; the meek who share in the very reign of God; and the hungry who are filled with every good thing. Mary's whole life is a living example of the power of the God who tells parables to confound the proud in their conceit and expose the powerlessness of the powerful.

God's Power On Behalf Of Justice

The three verses we are considering in this chapter highlight the history of Israel and the action of God on behalf of His people. The Hebrews were slaves in Egypt and endured great suffering. Yahweh was not indifferent to their cries for liberation and a new beginning. The faith of the people did not go unrewarded. The writer of Deuteronomy is well aware of what has been — slavery — and what God's power did for the Hebrews — deliverance:

> The Egyptians mistreated us; they tormented us and imposed a harsh slavery on us. We cried out to the Lord, the God who is our Father. The Lord listened to our cry and saw our torment, our labor, and our distress. He brought us out of Egypt with a strong hand and an outstretched arm, showing signs and wonders with awe-inspiring power. He brought us to this place and gave us this land, a land flowing with milk and honey. (Dt 26:6-9)

The action and power of God is on behalf of deliverance and liberation for His people who are being oppressed. God's power is revealed in His action on behalf of the powerless and the poor who have no worldly resources for strength. God must act for them or they will perish. The preaching of Jesus about the Kingdom is fundamentally about the God who acts with power. Whenever and wherever His children are in bondage (to the forces of economic, political, and social oppression as well as the spiritual oppression of sin) God's outstretched, mighty arm is at work on behalf of justice and liberation. The great English biblical scholar Norman Perrin has written: "The Kingdom of God is the power of God expressed in deeds; it is that which God does wherein it becomes evident that He is king. It is not a place or community ruled by God; it is not even the abstract idea or reign or kingship of God. It is quite concretely the activity of God as king" (*Rediscovering the Teaching of Jesus*).

Throughout the pages of Scripture, God's power (the power of His outstretched arm and the strength of His arm) is in action on behalf of the powerless, the weak, the voiceless, and the oppressed. God's activity in history is a clear laboring on behalf of justice for those who are being exploited and have no one to declare their cause. God is never indifferent to what goes on in His creation and the various ways His children act towards one another. The God who acts on behalf of justice for the poor demands that his people hear the cries of the oppressed. God not only acts on behalf of justice but first of all He *feels* the injustice of the world. That is, God responds because He is intimately and faithfully present to everything that happens. The hairs of our head are all counted and a sparrow does not fall without God's being aware and feeling its consequences. We have no watchmaker God who creates and then excuses Himself. God stays with His creation and works for a world in which justice (true peace based on generosity) is continually sought. While there is not perfect justice this side of the Kingdom, we must resist temptation and be open to hope. Not hope in our efforts alone, but in the power of God to be with us in our struggle for justice and liberation.

Process theologian Marjorie Hewitt Suchocki has written:

> Process theology suggests that the power of hope against despair is not paradoxical at all, but trusts in the nature of God as the power for justice. God is the source of the vision and of the reality; there is a locus for justice in the nature of God. The

effect of God upon us is the transmission of vision, along with the conviction of its worth and attainability. God is the source of hope. This is the significance of the doctrine of divine omnipotence for us. (*God Christ Church*, pp. 82-83)

Professor Suchocki's insight is crucial in our hungering and thirsting after justice. Her words about God warn against cynicism and fanaticism. The temptation to cynicism runs like this: poverty and injustice we will always have with us. No matter what we do, there will be sinful social structures. There are no quick fixes and instant solutions. In time moral fervor wanes and cynicism sets in. We go along in order to get along. There is also the temptation to fanaticism which is supported by a strong sense of self-righteousness and intolerance. Those who are not with us are against us — and must be converted or destroyed. In order to avoid cynicism and fanaticism we must seek justice in a spirit of confidence in God and hope in His power. Christian realism's laboring for justice acknowledges the limitations of all human efforts while being open to the power of God to do infinitely more than we can do by ourselves. Again the words of Professor Suchocki:

The reality of God's power relative to the world is such that there is ground to hope for the achievement of justice. This hope is due to the concrescent power of God as the locus of full justice in the transformation of the world, and to the faithfulness of God's influential power — God influences the world in keeping with the divine character, and thus leads the world toward modes of justice. If God is for us, who can be against us? And so we address the evils of our existence in the hope that they can be overcome. (*God Christ Church*, p. 89)

Sin: Impaired Vision

"What you see is what you get" is a common expression. However, we all know such is not the case. Seeing is never enough for living well and the development of moral character. We need more than sight. We need insight. The importance of insight or vision has been a crucial aspect of Western philosophy and theology. In Plato's allegory of the cave one painfully moves from the world of shadows to the light of the Good. Each step brings greater vision of the really real. In the Catholic tradition St. Thomas Aquinas holds that the ultimate end of the person is the Beatific Vision. Vision is never satisfied with surface appearances but seeks ever greater depth.

The Bible challenges a kind of surface living which results from not seeing the world properly. In fact, we can say that sin is impaired vision. We do not see our lives and the world around us in its proper way. Sin is distortion of action because our vision is distorted. Our character, that is our moral identity, is the result of how we see the world. Seeing the world rightly requires more than intellect and will power. Correct vision requires grace at work in a heart open to God's Spirit. Without the corrective aid of grace we always miss the mark and stumble on the illusions and idols we build. Iris Murdoch in her book, *Sovereignty of Good*, writes:

> By opening our eyes we do not necessarily see what confronts us. We are anxiety-ridden animals. Our minds are continually active, fabricating an anxious, usually self-preoccupied, often falsifying veil which partially conceals the world. (p. 84)

The high anxiety of the human condition blinds us to our true condition as creatures; our giftedness as children of the One who gives good things to all who ask; and the extent to which we depend on one another for life. Sin does not allow us to see any of this. Sin is blindness, distortion, and an illusion of our omnipotence. Sin is the false story and distorted vision that we are on our own. We are dependent on no one; hence we owe no one anything. The imperial ego continues to hold on to the center and bring everything and everyone into itself. Sin, as many theologians have attested, is not only individual but collective. There is a social dimension to blindness and arrogance. This is especially true of the modern State.

The blindness of nations is nothing new. The witness of the Bible clearly indicates that nations, even Israel, easily fall prey to the folly of sin's illusions: we are more because we have more; we are secure because we have more bombs and troops; we are superior because of our standard of living; and the list goes on and on. Consider Psalm 2:

Why do the nations conspire, and the peoples plot in vain? The kings of the earth set themselves up, and the rulers take counsel together, against the Lord and His anointed, saying, "Let us burst their bonds asunder, and cast their cords from us."

He who sits in the heavens laughs; the Lord has them in derision. . . Now therefore, O kings, be wise; be warned, O rulers of the earth. Serve the Lord with fear, with trembling kiss His feet, lest He be angry, and you perish in the way; for His wrath is quickly kindled.

Conde Pallen in his novel, *Crucible Island*, presents the State as the idol which demands our ultimate allegiance. The State brings us into being; nurtures us; and is purported to be our ultimate savior. Pallen presents what we might call a kind of catechism of the State as idol:

Q. - By whom were you begotten?
A. - By the Sovereign State.
Q. - Why were you begotten?
A. - That I might know, love, and serve the Sovereign State always.
Q. - What is the Sovereign State?
A. - The Sovereign State is humanity in composite and perfect being.
Q. - Why is the State supreme?
A. - The State is supreme because it is my Creator and Conserver in which I am and move and have my being and without which I am nothing.
Q. - What is the individual?
A. - The individual is only a part of the whole, and made for the whole, and finds his complete and perfect expression in the Sovereign State. Individuals are made for cooperation only, like feet, like hands, like eyelids, like the rows of the upper and lower teeth.

Perhaps the novel of Pallen seems a bit much. The State generally doesn't have all this power and control. Yet we must recognize that there is nothing more powerful and controlling than that which controls and comments without our awareness. We can be lulled into a fake sense of freedom. Herbert Schlossberg in his outstanding book, *Idol For Destruction*, writes:

Perhaps the most characteristic feature of modern history, one which impinges upon virtually every area of life, has been the development of the nation-state. So persuasive is its influence, so "normal" do its vast powers seem, that to read a document that seeks to limit severely the scope of those powers — even so recent a one as the Constitution of the United States — evokes a sense of great antiquity and strangeness. (p. 177)

The Magnificat clearly indicates that the proud and mighty (individually and collectively) suffer from a spiritual blindness —

proudness in the imagination — which prevents God's truth from taking root. Sin divides and alienates. Sin does not allow us to see the other as brother and sister; as Jesus in His need. We do not hear the cry of Lazarus outside our gate. We take no notice of the crumbs that fall from our table. Sin is selective attention and seeing. What is needed is a change — a conversion — of the imagination. If sin is blindness, salvation is vision.

That We May See

Sin blinds and distorts. The heart is turned in on itself. Insecurity and oppression result from a threatened ego and nation. Sin moves heart and nation to illusions of pride and power. Sin moves us to hold on to our thrones; believe we are good because we have been given (not earned in any final sense) good things; and seek after riches at the expense of the hungry. Yet no peace is found. The more we have the more we want. The achievements of others are threats to our own sense of self and well-being. Life becomes a see-saw: one can only rise if the other goes down, and *vice versa*. Enormous amounts of energy are spent staying on top, being #1.

The blindness of sin and the illusions of self-sufficiency are challenged by the gift of grace and the *true* power of salvation. Jesus comes to open our eyes and free our heart so that we can see and respond with love. Our character is formed by a new story, with new expectations, and a new vision of the true, good, and beautiful. In other words, in order to see properly, to have our vision corrected, we must allow our character to be formed within a community that tells the stories of Yahweh and Jesus. This is anything but automatic and effortless. We are formed by a specific content of images, symbols, and stories that help to structure our imagination and challenge all competing structures which claim to make us the center of things and in need of nothing. The outstanding moral ethicist Stanley Hauerwas writes:

The assumption seems to be that one's "vision" is relatively subjective and therefore cannot be analyzed or evaluated for its strength or weakness. Vision and utopianism are equated in a way that places one's ends beyond the scope of rational discussion. . . One simply assumes one's feelings of dissatisfaction are morally worthy and that the only issue is which political stance best exemplifies one's feelings. (*Vision and Virtue*, p. 227)

Professor Hauerwas has put his pen on a very important aspect of our vision and praxis for justice. Our vision, our story, is something deeper than a kind of motivistic response to what we see as injustice. There is about our vision and praxis a content which structures the way we look at reality and respond. Feelings and the massaging of our moral gland are never sufficient. They are not a lasting basis for character and a community of faith that does justice. We need something deeper. We need a grounding story which informs, challenges, and corrects. Again Professor Hauerwas:

This can be done by the Church [challenging all existing forms of social and political life which claim finality] because her loyalty is not centered in a cause of this world but in the final destiny of man, the kingdom of God, which has been revealed in Jesus Christ. (The fact that the Church's criterion of honesty is centered in Christ does not mean it necessarily has special insight in these matters. It must engage in the same kind of hard critical work that all men of good will must attempt in seeking understanding in these kinds of complex issues. The only difference is that the Church has no reason to fear the truth, no matter how destructive it may be.) The Church that serves such a truth may find itself the object of scorn as much

by the left as the center and right. (*Vision and Virtue*,
p. 228. Brackets added)

The grounding story (of Jesus as Lord and the destiny of
humankind as the Kingdom of God) does not only remain in the
mind (imagination). There is about the Christian story (revelation
as a way of seeing or vision) a call to action. The stories we tell and
retell are the stories we do again and again. Karl Marx criticized
philosophy for remaining removed from the concerns of flesh and
blood human beings. The Christian community should take note:
we tell stories of Yahweh and Jesus so that we can have vision and
act in a way that proclaims Jesus as Lord and the Kingdom as here
not yet. John A. Coleman, S.J. offers the following observation:

> The truth of the symbols of the Christian faith is more than a
> mere conceptual truth. Their truth lies in their power to make
> true. Christian symbols, in Dukheim's words, "transfigure the
> realities to which they relate." All of the Christian symbols are,
> in some sense, sacramental symbols. They are all directed to
> the primary sacraments of Christ and the Church, the centers
> of Christian life. They not only signify or mediate another
> reality but embody that reality and tansfigure the realities to
> which they relate. . . The Christian symbols exist less to help
> us to understand the world than to transform it. (*An American Strategic Theology*, p. 73)

The insights of Hauerwas and Coleman remind us of the need
for both vision *and* praxis or action. If we have only vision but no
action, then our stories are untested and we float in a make-believe,
utopian world. On the other hand, if we have action without vision
or a grounding story we can easily fall victim to fanaticism or
idolatry. We need a story or vision to keep us humble and we need
praxis (not a kind of pragmatism which only looks to results or what

is most effective or successful) in order to test the adequacy of our vision.

Mary: The Woman Of Vision And Praxis

In the life of Mary we see the power of God's grace working through human weakness. Mary is to be counted by the world (the principalities and powers that continually contest the authority of God over His creation) as one of low degree and, like her Son, having nothing that would cause the world to take note. For the principalities and powers of this eon can only see that which finds power in money, popularity, and worldly clout. The deeper workings of the Spirit go unnoticed — or if noticed, they must be fought in order to maintain the illusion of self-sufficiency and autonomy.

The imagination and heart of Mary are centered in God — totally. From the moment of her existence Mary's life was oriented toward doing the will of God. Her vision was formed in the womb and continued to mature throughout her life. Mary's Immaculate Conception was received into God through her Assumption into heaven. A total life for God could only be perfected in God's total acceptance of Mary. What God had done for Mary from the beginning was continued right into eternity. Mary's total life signifies the total *fidelity of God* for His world and people. And here is the crucial vision that guides Mary's life: unlike the blindness and illusion of sin which moves the ego to the center of things, Mary continually does the will of God in her own quiet and uncelebrated way. Her story is God's story of the mighty things His outstretched arm has accomplished. There is nothing she does that is separate from God's will. We see in Mary a woman of great strength and freedom. She has no need to play the power game of control, recognition, and celebrity. And it is because Mary has given up playing the games of this world that she becomes honored for all generations. Mary's whole life was one of considering God. God was continually mindful of Mary. The tragedy of sin is the failure to see that God is mindful of us. In many ways we build hell here and in eternity by going on our own and being mindful only of ourselves. Karl Barth wrote:

> All of us, probably, are such mighty ones and must be put down from our thrones if we want to have anything to do with God. How does God do this "putting down from the throne," and how will it become true also in world history?. . . We need not think of something big and loud and external. . . God's ways are always *hidden*, quiet ways. What happens here is not dramatic, but all the more wondrous. It is only required that God turns away, does *not* consider us anymore as he regarded Mary. Being put down from our thrones quite simply happens, I believe, in this way — that God turns away from us — and that is the most terrible thing that God can do to us, simply let us proceed. . . Let us not by any means imagine hell as a place where one is permanently beaten or roasted. There will be gathered indeed great lords and nice people, but great lords and nice people without God. (*The Great Promise*, pp. 52-3)

CHAPTER

5

Memory And Justice

"He has helped His servant Israel, in remembrance of His
mercy, as He spoke to our fathers, to Abraham and to
his posterity forever." (Lk 1:55)

The closing words of the Magnificat remind us of the most
important insights of biblical spirituality: God *acts* in human
history. The God of Abraham and his descendants does not remain
indifferent to the work of His hands. God creates and He cares.
God's active word calls all things into being and He is involved in
all that unfolds. Far from being an absent or spectator God,
Yahweh is ever mindful of what takes place on earth. History is
more than the passing of events. History is going someplace and it
is going to be fulfilled in someone. History is moving toward the
Kingdom of God and when Jesus comes in glory at the *parousia*
then He will be all in all. What we do as individuals, communities,
and nations makes a difference to God. The words of the Lord's
Prayer say it powerfully: "Thy kingdom come, Thy will be done
on earth as it is in heaven."

Before going further in exploring the importance of history for those who claim to be followers of Yahweh and Jesus, we must be ever mindful that God acts in history and is concerned in its outcome, for our philosophical and modern views of history reject or remain indifferent to the biblical view. For Plato, time and history were to be escaped through contemplation of the eternal forms. Time was man's enemy. Time, temporality, spoke of our finitude, limitations, sufferings, and finally death. Only with death could the soul hope to escape the body (a prison which needed to be constantly disciplined) and be absorbed in the objective immortality of God (Mind or Over-Soul).

In modern time the renowned German philosopher G.W.F. Hegel believed that all history was essentially the story of the human mind or consciousness. It is man alone who is able to make sense and find meaning in his past, present, and future. In his outstanding book, *Death of a Soul*, William Barrett comments: ''The Greeks spoke of man as the rational animal; following Hegel, perhaps we should speak of man as the historical animal.'' This awareness of history (especially how we humans are so absorbed in time and limited by time) has had profound effects in the field of modern theology.

The great philosopher and theologian Bernard Lonergan, S.J. teaches that the major shift in consciousness or mind is the shift from the classical consciousness to an historical one. Classical thought emphasized the unchanging, immutable, eternal, and substantial. Modern consciousness emphasizes the experience of change, growth, process, and motion. This historical consciousness or mind-set has ushered in some profound consequences for theology and ethics. The unchanging dogmas and teachings of the Church are examined in light of the historical, social, and cultural factors which gave rise to them. The absolute norms of morality do not seem quite so absolute. The historical consciousness views reality in a very *conditioned* way. In addition, the human person is an *active* participant in the unfolding story of history. Naturally the historical consciousness forces the question: if a teaching or moral norm can be shown to have resulted from certain historical factors, why can't *all* dogmas and norms be so challenged and changed? The rise of historical consciousness at the same time places greater responsibility on the human person for his beliefs and actions. Mere repetition is deemed "bad-faith." The Jesuit theologian Avery Dulles has written extensively on the relationship between historical consciousness and dogma:

> It is difficult for a contemporary Christian, living in close contact with the world about him, to accept Christianity with the same kind of faith that he himself or his parents would have possessed thirty or fifty years ago. What is not too clear, from the empirical evidence, is the nature of the present crisis. Is it that Christian faith is itself becoming more difficult to attain? Or is it simply that the cultural forms in which Christianity has become clothed have ceased to be appropriate today? We must inquire whether the present crisis of faith may not be due in part to the transition from older styles of expression to forms more suited to our time. If such is the true interpretation of the present crisis, we need not regret that it is occuring. (*The Survival Of Dogma*, p. 17). (Also see Dulles' *A Church To Believe In*)

Finally, in a reaction against finding in history some ultimate meaning, "social or objective" historical works do not look for patterns or goals to events but simply record episodes as a kind of mindless behaviorism. Following the lead of behavioristic psychology, social history is nothing but a record of various external factors which influence and control the responses of the individual and nations. The causes and explanations of history are to be found solely in *this* world. There is no transcendental meaning or goal to time. Time is aimless and meaningless.

The biblical understanding of history stands in contrast to these philosophical and modern views. Hegel, to be sure, presents man as the historical being whose consciousness unfolds with the passage of time. The Bible goes further. History is much deeper than the unfolding of the human mind. It is the stage on which God reveals Himself to us and we respond to God's self-revelation. This response to God is either one of belief or disbelief. The nation of Israel does not merely have a philosophy of history which speaks of its meaningfulness and its goal. She has a *theology* of history. God is involved with and acts for Israel. Renowned biblical scholar John L. McKenzie, S.J. writes:

> Israel, then, had a concept of history; when we examine the concept, it turns out to be the fruit of what we would call a theology of history. The unity and continuity of the historical process comes from Israel's recognition of itself not only as a people, but as the people of Yahweh. Its history is the history of its encounter with Yahweh and of its response to the encounter. Its interest is cosmic because there is only one God and one historical process. And history is a process, a development through crisis, a development in which Yahweh is more clearly recognized in His true reality. . . The purpose of Israel . . . was to present a true picture of the reality of God operating in history and of man's response to God's operation; this to them was "historical truth," and they must be judged on this basis and not on their success or failure in recounting "historical facts." (*Dictionary of the Bible,* pp. 362-63)

God In Search Of Man

The importance of historical consciousness and the historical reality of our being says some profound things about God. For if man is the historical being, the being in time, then God's involvement with man must be historical as well. In the words of the Magnificat: ''All generations will call me blessed''; ''His mercy is on those who fear Him from generation to generation''; and ''He has helped His servant Israel, in remembrance of His mercy, as He spoke to our fathers, to Abraham and to his posterity forever.'' The Magnificat is quite profound in its understanding of God's action on behalf of His people. There is a sophisticated blending of the historical and the eternal. God is a dynamic, active, and responding Lover who always seeks to meet the real needs of His people. Hence God's grace is historical — in time. At the same time, God's love is eternal. It lasts from generation to generation and to the children of Abraham forever.

The historical aspect of God's involvment and the eternal reality of His love offers us a breath-taking story of God: He is *never* indifferent or unmoved by our suffering, hurts, cries, or needs. Neither is God unmindful of the plight of the poor and the wretched. He is especially concerned about those who find only ''a heartless world.'' Yahweh is close to the broken-hearted. The biblical experience of God is quite different from Greek philosophy and psychology. The Greeks valued stability, the immovable, the unchangeable, and that which is beyond the flux of time. God is the Unmoved Mover. Nothing below can really affect God in His heaven. By contrast, the God of Abraham has the strength to be moved and affected by His people. God is a passionate, loving God who desires His people to respond to His self-disclosures. The power of God is the ability to change endlessly in His *responses* to the cries and sufferings of His people. Far from being the Unmoved Mover, God is ''the Most Moved Mover.'' In saying this — that God changes in His responses to His people — there is no loss of divine power (it is helpful to remember what A.N. Whitehead once said — God does not need our metaphysical compliments). Theologian John C. Merkle captures the immutable and changing aspects of God:

> The fact that God's modes of reacting to the world are changeable does not mean that God changes in essence. To be in essence passible is not the same as to have a possible

essence. To be in essence passible is to be by nature a being who may change modes of action and reaction;. . . God's nature may be immutable while the modes of God's being-in-relation may change. Specifically, while God *is* the transcendent, transitive concern for being, the expressions of that concern are historical and subject to change. (*The Genesis of Faith*, p. 133)

The Bible says a most shocking thing: God searches for us. And God will never be satisfied until we respond to His gestures of love and self-giving. Our God is anything but a World Spirit, First Cause, Unmoved Mover, or Mind filled with Eternal Forms. God is moved by our actions and needs. Our cries for help are always heard. Our acts and structures of injustice and brutality do not go without divine judgment. God is the Hound of Heaven who seeks *us* continually. The parables of Jesus in the Gospel of Luke clearly present God in search of us. Chapter 5 of Luke contains three images of God in pursuit of wayward man. God is like a shepherd who goes in search of a stray sheep and leaves the others untended. When the stray is found the shepherd (God) rejoices. God is like a *woman* (!) who loses one coin and will not rest until she finds it. She spends a great deal of time and oil in the search. Once again when the lost is found, there *must* be rejoicing. And finally, God is like a father who must let go of a son so he can come to his senses. When he does and returns home the father (God) runs from the house and celebrates, for the dead son has come back to life.

The God who searches for us is far removed from the God of the philosophers. Here is a God who is simply mad by the standards of human reason. Here is a God who refuses to wait on us but actively tugs at our heart until we respond. Ours is not a ceremonious God of pomp and circumstance. The God of Abraham and the Father of Jesus (ours too) is not afraid to get involved in our messy history and all too human condition (the Word becomes our poor flesh in history). The story of God told by Luke is one of unbounded joy and a love for us that far exceeds our wildest dreams. Father Andrew Greeley, commenting on the parables in Luke and the story of God which emerges, reminds us:

> The fundamental assumption of Christianity is that God is mad. At least by human standards, the Deity behaves in an embarrassingly berserk fashion. . . One can go through many more of the parables of Jesus and discover the same theme — the absurd, insane generosity of God. Our God is an embarrassing sort of God. He doesn't behave with dignity. . . He doesn't want our sacrifices . . . our virtuous devotion. . . He wants us. And that is undignified to Him and disturbing to us for we would much prefer to have a God who is satisfied with fasting and sacrifices, a presentable, reasonable, sensible God. (*The Touch of the Spirit*, pp. 9-12)

The God of the Magnificat and the God of the parables of Jesus are one and the same. God is a passionate, loving God who is ever mindful of His children. His love is capable of maddening generosity from generation to generation. The generous love of God finds special meaning for the poor, lowly, voiceless, powerless, and the sinner. God searches for man in those places which seem most distant and lost. God actively pursues the wretched of the earth so as to place them on the vacant thrones of the worldly powerful. The God who searches for lamb, coin, and son gone astray is the same God who selects Mary to be His special handmaid and servant. And what God has done must be remembered from generation to generation; from Abraham to his posterity forever.

Mitsvah

The closing lines of the Magnificat are steeped in the Jewish faith. Essential to the Jewish faith is the notion of *mitsvah* — the good and holy deed. The Jewish faith and tradition are kept alive by memory. The community must continually call to mind the good and holy deeds of Yahweh on behalf of His people. The community continues and *grows* in faith by recalling again and again what God has done for the people. Without this memory of the good and holy deeds of God, faith dies and the holiness of God remains a secret. The world and the people go on their ways *as if* God did not exist.

The holy and good deeds of Yahweh are of two major groups: the mighty deeds of God on behalf of His people in history, and secondly, the presence of God in the life of the individual believer. God acts in history on behalf of Israel; this action takes the qualities of commitment and liberation. God has chosen this collection of tribes to be His people. He will form a covenant with them and remain forever faithful. No matter what Israel does, God will never be unfaithful. He will become angry, jealous, and even allow them to be taken into exile. However, through it all God continues to be their God and Israel His people. The God who brought them out of the bondage of Egypt continues to liberate His people from the slavery of idolatry and social injustice. For slavery is deeper than political bondage and exile. Sin is the slavery which leads to death; the ultimate exile is banishment from God. Each new generation must once again be committed to the Lord's covenant and experience His liberating power. Covenant commitment cannot be taken for granted. Our ancestors in faith can share and pass on the tradition; it is up to each new generation to make the tradition a part of its life story.

As it is in the collective memory of Israel so it must be in the heart of each believer — special moments of the holy and good deeds of God. Each of us can call to mind special episodes of God's care and grace. Granted such moments of grace are all too rare and our awareness of them all too dim — but they do occur. In one of his most famous sermons Paul Tillich put it this way:

Do we know what it means to be struck by grace? It does *not* mean that we suddenly believe that God exists . . . grace does not mean simply that we are making progress in our moral self-control . . . and certainly it does *not* happen if we try to force it upon ourselves. . . Grace strikes us when we are in great pain and restlessness. It strikes us when we walk through the dark valley of a meaningless and empty life. It strikes us when we feel that our separation is deeper than usual. . . It strikes us when our disgust for our own being . . . and lack of direction and composure have become intolerable to us. . . Sometimes at that moment a wave of light breaks into our darkness, and it is as though a voice were saying: "You are accepted. *You are accepted,* accepted by that which is greater than you, and the name of which you do not know. Do not ask for the name now; perhaps you will find it later. . . Simply accept the fact that you are accepted!" (*The Shaking of the Foundations*, pp. 161-2)

These powerful words of Tillich find a soul-mate in the words of Abraham Joshua Heschel. In his book, *Man is not Alone*, Rabbi Heschel invites us to cherish those special moments when the presence of God breaks into the everydayness of our lives. We humans are so easily distracted and wrapped up in our projects and concerns. We compulsively build idols and too often live by the illusions of self-sufficiency and omnipotence. However, we come to deep truths about our existence to the extent that we remember and befriend those sacred moments of God's intense being-with-us. Heschel writes:

In every man's life there are moments when there is a lifting of the veil at the horizon of the known, opening a sight of the eternal. Each of us has at least once in his life experienced the momentous reality of God. . . But such experiences or inspirations are rare events. To some people they are like shooting stars, passing and unremembered. In others they kindle a light that is never quenched. The remembrance of that experience and the loyalty to the response of that moment are the forces that sustain faith. In this sense, *faith is faithfulness*, loyalty to an event, loyalty to our response. (*Man is not Alone*, p. 165)

How do we grow in the ability to be aware of God's presence? And furthermore, how do we continue to remember the good and holy deeds of God? Awareness of and fidelity to the faithful love of God requires several things of us. We need the community of faith which tells and retells the stories of God. Again and again we must hear the narratives about what God has done, continues to do, and we hope will do in the future. The telling of stories within the community forms a character which seeks to connect the stories proclaimed to the story of one's life.

In addition to a living tradition or body of stories which help form character, we need to re-experience and remember the good and holy deeds of God through liturgy or ritual. Through the appropriate use of word, action, and symbol we call to mind and become one with the mighty deeds of God. The holy and good deeds of God are taken out of space and time, and we in our space and time, so as to form a *present* reality. God's action of creation, liberation, mercy, salvation, and healing are *not* frozen in time but *continue* to be made present again and again to each new generation. It is *we* who are *now* liberated and healed. We know, in an experiential way, God's mighty arm of salvation and graciousness. Ritual and liturgical celebration call to mind and heart what God has done. But just as important, liturgy and ritual remind us that God is at work in our lives and the history of the community. Memory is never just the passive calling to mind of past events. It is the active living and awareness of God being God in the here and now of heart and history.

Finally, *mitsvah* calls for action on our part. To remember the good and holy deeds of God means that we are called to do good and holy deeds in our lives. The more one does, the more one becomes. That is, in doing acts of justice and mercy we become like the God of justice and mercy. The concern of God for the poor, powerless, rejected, enslaved, and wretched must be shared by those who are part of the covenant of remembrance. God's continual, abiding love and generosity for the poor and brokenhearted is carried by His people. Each person becomes a living sacrament — a revelation — of God's merciful, caring love. It is through our working for justice, freedom, and peace that the divine becomes present and visible in the midst of the secular. If we do not remember, we cannot act. And if there is no action for justice and mercy, then we no longer remember what God did. Commenting on the need to remember and do the good and holy deeds of God, we again need to consider the words of John C. Merkle:

> If the divine is absent from our world, if our lives are dreadfully unredeemed, we must not blame God. God creates a world sublime, but we fail to appreciate it; a world full of mystery that we mistake for absurdity. The glory of God fills the earth, but we do our best to conceal it; God's will has been revealed to the prophets, interpreted by the sages, conveyed by the tradition, but we fail to remember it. God assaults our conscience with the demands for justice and love, and we ignore the outcry. Accusing God for being absent, as if we have been present; blaming God for the ills that plague us, as if we have been laboring to redeem the world, is not the way . . . To do a *mitsvah* is to bring God back from exile. . . And by bringing God back into our deeds, into our lives, we advance the work of redemption. This, in the end, is the goal of faith: to make our lives and our world more compatible with the glory of God. (*The Genesis of Faith*, pp. 216-17)

The great acts of mercy, love, and generosity which Yahweh had shown to Israel have once again been visited on God's new servant — Mary. Mary understands her story of faith within the larger context or narrative of Yahweh's relationship with Israel. St. Luke tells us in the verse following the Magnificat that Mary stayed with Elizabeth for three months. In a very matter-of-fact fashion Luke is telling us that the woman who remembers the good and holy deeds of God *does* these deeds of goodness, mercy, and love. Happy will we be if remember to do the same.

The Dangerous Mary

The stories of Yahweh and Jesus form a dangerous memory. Why? Because the telling and living of these stories challenge us to change and confront *all* political, social, and economic systems which try to claim absolute authority or goodness. To remember what God did and continues to do in history serves as a lasting critique of all human pretensions to replace the Kingdom of God. To remember the liberating activity of God in the events of Exodus and the Paschal Mystery of Jesus keeps the future open until He comes again. We can never be satisfied with the status quo. The dangerous memory that is kept alive from generation to generation is one that is simply *subversive*. Secular and worldly principalities and powers are challenged as usurpers. The collective self-righteousnesss and manifest destiny of all political orders are called to repentance and conversion — again and again. Father Johann Baptist Metz has written the following about the dangerous memory of Jesus Christ:

> . . . there are dangerous memories, memories which make demands on us. There are memories in which earlier experiences break through to the center-point of our lives and reveal new and dangerous insights for the present. They illuminate for a few moments and with a harsh steady light the questionable nature of things we have apparently come to terms with, and show up the banality of our supposed 'realism.' They

break through the canon of the prevailing structures of plausibility and have certain subversive features. Such memories are like dangerous and incalculable visitations from the past. They are memories that we have to take into account, memories, as it were, with a future content. (*Faith in History and Society*, pp. 109-110)

What is the content of this memory that makes it so dangerous? The community of faith continues to proclaim the dangerous memory of Jesus as incarnate, crucified, and risen. The Word made flesh is the ultimate act of God's commitment to the human person. Our God entered completely into our human condition so that the ultimate enemies of man — sin and death — can be conquered. Our absolute allegiance belongs to the God who loves absolutely and eternally. God becoming our poor flesh is the never-to-be-taken-back pledge of love. All of our loves, commitments, and allegiances must be understood in light of that one final, complete allegiance — fidelity to God's new covenant in Jesus Christ. To substitute a human creation for the Creator is idolatry. We will only know true and lasting peace when we give our total allegiance to the God who gave Himself totally to us in Jesus. The memory of the Incarnation is dangerous to all earthly powers which seek to control and dominate life as if they were in charge. Our dangerous memory proclaims that true power is to be found in the Word that enfleshed itself in one of the "poor of Yahweh."

The Word that becomes our poor flesh does not avoid the brokenness of our human condition and history. God takes on the sinfulness, banality, and evil that is so much a part of our history. The Christian story proclaims from generation to generation the Crucified and Abandoned One on Golgotha. The One whom we proclaim to be Lord was rejected, despised, convicted, and condemned by the so-called respectable forces of religion and government. The Crucified One stands a constant reminder to the Church and all Christians of the need to be prophetic when it comes to the pretensions of earthly powers. We understand history very differently from the way in which those who sit on mighty thrones do. They see history as the story of the powerful, the established, the successful. By contrast, the Christian understands history from the perspective of the Cross. We must be in solidarity with victims since the Crucified One, whom we proclaim as Lord, is the Innocent, Suffering Victim. God became our poor flesh to the point of dying a real death. The death of Jesus came at the hands of the mighty. And it is the mighty who continue to challenge God's rule by placing their trust in things.

The Crucified One is also the Risen Lord. The Christian story does not end on Good Friday with the rock-covered tomb. It proclaims a Good Friday because there is an Easter Sunday and the empty tomb. The One who was rejected by the world has found favor with the Father. The scandal of the Cross has been transformed into the victory of life over death; love over fear; and hope over despair. The Christian community is a community of hope which looks through the brokenness of the present and sees the workings of the Spirit. Like Mary, we may not fully understand how all of life will turn out. But faith means that we do not fully understand. We trust in the One who has proved to be worthy of our trust. The resurrection of Jesus does not do away with His sufferings. Rather, the sufferings of Jesus help us to understand suffering and death in a new way. They no longer have the final word. Father Metz puts it this way:

> I believe that such a resurrection faith is expressed inasmuch as it acts 'contra-factually' in making us free to bear in mind the sufferings and hopes of the past and the challenge of the dead. It allows not only a revolution that will change the things of tomorrow for future generations, but a revolution that will decide anew the meaning of our dead and their hopes. Resurrection mediated by way of the memory of suffering means: The dead, those already vanquished and forgotten, have a

meaning which is yet unrealized. The potential meaning of our history does not depend only on the survivors, the successful and those who make it. Meaning is not a category that is only reservedly for the conquerors! (*Faith in History and Society*, pp. 113-114)

The dangerous memory of the Christian about the God who is Incarnate, Crucified, and Risen challenges all political and social arrangements which claim to be ultimate and forget the suffering-poor. The Christian story has about it an ultimate hope that does come from the work of our hands but is a gift from our gracious God. The memory of the Christian carries forward to meet the Kingdom of the God who is Absolute Future. The Christian never retreats into a private world of "Thee and Me." To be caught up in the memory of the Christian story stretches our hearts and widens our vision so that we see the Crucified and Risen One in the wretched and forgotten. The social structures which organize so much of our lives can never be left on their own to do what they will. The Christian story clings, from generation to generation, to a vision of the Kingdom in which lasting justice, freedom, and peace will be realized. Until that time we follow the example of Mary: we treasure this memory in our hearts; we share this dangerous memory with the posterity of Abraham forever; and this memory of the Generous God who became one with us and for us sustains us in our hungering and thirsting for justice.

Mary Ever Virgin

We began our reflections on Mary and social justice by taking account of the seeming contradiction between the two. Mary has been misportrayed as a kind of goddess devoid of human attractiveness and even challenging Yahweh and Jesus for our devotion. Advocates of social justice have often seen Mary as an obstacle to concern for the poor and powerless. She became a symbol for all that is wrong with a vertical-only religion — private, individualized, and concerned with saving souls devoid of bodies. It is hoped that the reflections in this book have corrected these erroneous views of Mary. Mary is so attractive because she is so human. Mary is the glory of God because she is so fully alive with His presence and word. She is the woman for others. The Magnificat clearly indicates how much Mary has to offer for our faith that seeks justice.

A brief closing word needs to be said about another misunderstood aspect of Mary, namely, her virginity. We can state the teaching of the Catholic Church concerning Mary's virginity in a kind of Cartesian "clear and distinct" idea: Mary, the Mother of God, was a virgin in the conception of her child, and she remained a virgin after his birth for the rest of her earthly existence. Having said all of this, we need to proceed to a deeper level of reflection: What does Mary's virginity mean for the Church and our individual

Christian life? In addition, we need to ask what the virginity of Mary tells us about God. And finally, what is the connection between virginity and social justice?

It is important to keep in mind that virginity, like poverty, is not an end in itself. There is nothing virtuous or holy about poverty or virginity in themselves. In fact, virginity was not deemed an honor or a state of holiness but a condition of dishonor. For example in Judges 11:38 we read: "And he said, 'Go,' and he sent her away for two months; and she departed, she and her companions, and bewailed her virginity upon the mountains." The daughter of Jepthah is greatly distressed by the thought of never being married or knowing the joy of having children. This is because at the end of those two months her father killed her as a human sacrifice. Israel, the people of Yahweh, is often spoken of as the "Virgin Daughter of Zion." The virginity of Zion (Israel) is a cause of great anxiety, for she may perish before the coming (birth) of the Messiah. This anxiety is only heightened by the realization that the Messiah is the Promised One who will bring liberation and deliverance.

In the Gospel of St. Luke we read that a virgin named Mary is visited by God's messenger. Gabriel tells Mary that she is highly favored and will conceive a son called Jesus. This child will be the Son of the Most High and usher in the definitive reign of God. Mary is troubled and anxious about the message: "How shall this be, since I do not know man?" The answer is most profound: "The Holy Spirit will come upon you, and the power of the Most High will overshadow you; therefore the child to be born will be called holy, the Son of God." St. Luke continues his Gospel of reversing our human expectations. The God of Scripture takes what has been a reproach and turns it into a song (The Magnificat). Theologian Max Thurian has written:

> The Virgin Mary who gives birth to the Messiah is the Daughter of Zion, but her virginity is no longer a matter of

shame since she has become fruitful by the operation of the Spirit. On the contrary, indeed, this virginity is the sign of the intimacy between God and Mary. Further than that, according to Judaic tradition of the time, she is in the line of Sarah who gave birth 'according to the Spirit,' of Moses and Zipporah, separated by the unique calling of God at the burning bush, and of the 'Sons of Light' associated with the angels in the conflict of the last days. . . (*Mary, Mother of all Christians*, p. 28)

The virginity of Mary is not to be understood as a reproach, and neither is it to be understood (as in more recent times) as an anti-sexual bias by the Scriptures or the Church. Granted the influence of certain aspects of Greek thought along with an anti-body mentality on the part of some religious writers, could easily lead one to conclude that virginity and celibacy are upheld as a way of downgrading human sexuality. However, it cannot be emphasized enough that such views of virginity and human sexuality are distortions. What the virginity of Mary says, especially from the perspective of St. Luke, is that she was singled out by God for a unique role in salvation history. The special relationship of Mary to God is one of deepest intimacy. The angel Gabriel is sent to announce to Mary that she will be the one to provide the "human face" for the Word who is about to enter our human condition and history. The virginity of Mary does not come at the expense of God but comes as a great sign of His generous love and Mary's special role. J.H. Nicolas, O.P. has written:

The grandeur and beauty of virginity in no way means that marriage is to be deprecated or human love despised. It asserts its own excellence without any detriment to other essential values, even when it may be preferred to them. . . The radiant image of the blessed Woman, who by the paths of perfect virginity, was led to the highest and most complete form of

Motherhood has thus done much to reveal to men the true sense of virginity, which is not mutilation or limitation, but on the contrary shows a positive and expansive quality. (*The Virginity of Mary*)

The virginity of Mary speaks a timely and timeless message. The individual Christian and the community of faith are singled out and raised up by God in order to *continue* the work of the Virgin Mary. Individually and collectively we are to let God's Word become enfleshed in us so that we can bring Christ to the world. We are to be Christ-bearers as Mary was. We are to be open to receive the message and the power of the Holy Spirit. The Incarnation, uniquely unfolded in Mary, is not frozen in space and time. The Church throughout the centuries continues to let the Almighty overshadow her so that He who is mighty can continue to do great things. In a very profound sense the Church and the Christian are called to be virginal regardless of one's calling to the married, single, or religious life. George A. Maloney, S.J. in his book *Mary: The Womb of God* writes:

Mary understood by the power of the Holy Spirit . . . that everything about her came from God as a gift. . . Because she was so not only spiritually but also physically . . . she stands as the archetype of the Church in the thinking and prayer life of the early Church.

The Church, like Mary, receives all of its unique meaning as total gift of grace from God. There is nothing from this world. The Church is the Body of Christ, meant to form His life in its members, but through grace, life from above, from God and not "of the will of man." (pp. 43-44)

Renowned theologian Hugo Rahner, S.J. understood the Incarnation as the prime mission of the Church. Hence, when we speak about Mary we are talking about the Church. Father Rahner writes:

> Here indeed is the great mystery of the Church: the union of the divine and human nature in the womb of the Virgin. . . If the Church is to remain faithful to her vocation . . . there must always be these 'chosen souls' who follow Mary in what she was, and show the way to what the blessed will be in heaven. (*Our Lady and the Church*, p. 32)

Father Rahner is reminding us that the mission of the Christian and community is to be a point of disclosure and union between God and our human nature. There are those who are called to be physically virginal. Others will be called to the married state. Yet all of God's people are called to "show the way" by being a virgin, that is, one whose whole life is understood as a gift. And it is only in God that we come to know true and lasting peace.

The virginity of Mary is an eloquent testimony about God. As with all aspects of Mary's life, her virginity ultimately points to the Almighty who has done great things. Throughout the Magnificat we are told a story of God in which divine generosity is showered on our humanity. Ours is a gracious God who is ever mindful of the needs of His children. The mindfulness of God is especially keen for the poor, weak, powerless, and wretched of the earth. This lowly and obscure virgin has found favor with the God whose favor overflows with good things. Mary, whose life has been un-celebrated and unnoticed by the movers and shakers, is highly favored by God and will be celebrated from generation to generation. And in celebrating Mary we are giving praise to the God who acts in powerful and unexpected ways. Out of the most impossible situations God calls forth new possibilities. In those lives which seem to be life-less, God is able to bring forth new life.

In bringing our reflections to a close, we need to say a brief word about the relationship between virginity and the concerns of social justice. Mary is a wonderfully strong human being who is able to freely admit her true condition: she is of low estate. This is not a statement of self-hatred or false humility but a declaration of her full dependence upon the Lord. Mary is humble because she is a woman of truth. Mary knows that all she is and will become is the result of God's grace at work in her. The virginity of Mary highlights the true poverty of our human condition and our need to be totally dependent upon God's gift of grace.

The virginity of Mary reminds those on their mighty thrones, and those who occupy the citadels of power, that one can only rely on God. To try and find lasting happiness in things, achievements, power, or human relationships is an illusion. To be truly centered in God is to *do* the good and just works of God. Like God, we are called to give food to the hungry, clothing to the naked, visit the sick and imprisoned, and make welcome the stranger. None of this is possible if we understand reality in terms of having, achieving, and acquiring. If, however, like Mary we wait upon the Lord then it is in giving that we receive. For there is nothing that we truly give that has not first been given to us. And there is, furthermore, nothing that we share with others that will not be multiplied by the gracious love of the God who knows what we need before we even ask.

We shall end our reflections with a prayer by a seventeenth century Reformed pastor, Charles Delancourt:

O Almighty God, who, by thine infinite and incomprehensible power didst draw from man (Adam) the mother of the living (Eve) without the aid of woman, according to the rich treasures of thine inexhaustible wisdom, thou hast thought it fitting to fashion the Prince of Life in the substance of a woman without any work of man. A woman had borne for us the fruit of death and here we behold another who presents us with the fruit of life and immortality.

O Lord, whose will it was to be born of a virgin, but of a virgin betrothed, to honour thy one same act with both virginity and marriage, and to obtain for thy mother both a support and a witness and innocence. . .

There, O Lord, by a handful of virgin earth, thou didst form Adam in thy image and likeness and didst clothe him with justice and holiness, but here with virgin blood thou hast formed the new Adam, who is thy living image, the splendour of thy glory, and the graven record of thy person. (Quoted by Max Thurian in *Mary, Mother of all Christians*, pp. 40-41)

Further Readings

In addition to the books mentioned previously, the following are offered as further reading on themes discussed in the text.

Brown, Raphael. *The Life of Mary as Seen by the Mystics* (Bruce Publishing Co., 1951).

Buby, Bertrand. *Mary, The Faithful Disciple* (Paulist Press, 1985).

Deiss, Lucien. *Mary, Daughter of Sion* (Liturgical Press, 1972).

Demarest, Donald and Gaylor, Coley. *The Dark Virgin: The Book of Our Lady of Guadalupe* (Academy Guild Press, 1956).

Engelsman, Jean Chamberlain. *The Feminine Dimension of the Divine* (Westminster, 1979).

Heyward, Isabel and Ochs, Carol. *Women and Spirituality* (Recoman and Allanheld, 1983).

Kung, H. and Moltman, J. *Mary in the Churches* (Concilium, 168. Seabury and Winston, 1983).

Metz, Johann B. *The Emergent Church* (Crossroads, 1981).

Ruether, Rosemary. *Religion and Sexism* (Simon and Schuster, 1974).

Sheed, F.J. *The Mary Book* (Sheed and Ward, 1951).

Tambasco, Anthony J. *What Are They Saying About Mary?* (Paulist Press, 1984).

Thurian, Max. *Mary Mother of the Lord/Figure of the Church* (The Faith Press, 1963).

Vollert, Cyril. *A Theology of Mary* (Herder and Herder, 1965).

Additional MARIAN publications and tapes from ALBA HOUSE

MARY, QUEEN OF PEACE
by Rev. Robert Faricy, S.J. and Sister Lucy Rooney, S.N.D.
". . . Father Robert Faricy and Sister Lucy Rooney, two Americans who are now respected teachers in Rome, have been to Medjugorje several times. They . . . have examined a great deal of evidence, and they tell what they found in their book, *Mary, Queen of Peace* . . . It includes descriptions of what the authors saw in Medjugorje and a transcript of a conversation between a priest and one of the children who claim to see and speak with the Mother of Jesus." *New Covenant* $4.95

TWO MONTHS WITH MARY
Short Reflections for Every Day of May and October
by Joseph A. Viano, S.S.P.
The thoughts for each day of the month of May concentrate on the truths we all hold dear regarding Mary as the Mother of God and the Mother of us all. The thoughts for October honor her as the Queen of the Rosary and offer reflections on the mysteries of this powerful devotion. $3.95

ROSARY: A GOSPEL PRAYER
by Wilfrid J. Harrington, O.P.
In this excellent book, Fr. Harrington shows that the great Marian prayer will always be a treasured Church devotion. Those who have remained faithful to it will be overjoyed to find that they have not remained faithful in vain and the younger generation will discover here fascinating insights guaranteed to make them feel that the Rosary is more worthwhile than ever.   Over 20,000 sold! $2.95